D1879363

GOODBYE TO TAMIL MOTHERLAND

GOODBYE TO TAMIL MOTHERLAND

THE RISE OF LABOUR MIGRATION OVERSEAS AND THE SOCIETY, 1729-1890

S. JEYASEELA STEPHEN

GenNext Publication

© **Author**

All rights reserved. No part of this work may be reproduced, stored, adapted, or transmitted in any form or by any means, electronic, mechanical, photocopying, micro-filming, recording or otherwise, or translated in any language, without the prior written permission of the copyright owner and the publisher. The book is sold subject to the condition that it shall not, by way of trade or otherwise, be lent, resold, hired out, or otherwise circulated without the prior publisher's written consent in any form of binding or cover other than that in which it is published.

The views and opinions expressed in this book are author(s) own and the facts reported by them have been verified to the extent possible, and the publishers are not in any way liable for the same.

ISBN 978-93-8022-348-3

First Published, 2019

Published by

GenNext Publication
5, Ansari Road
Daryaganj, New Delhi-110002
Phone: 9811692060
E-mail: gennextpublication@hotmail.com

Printed at: G. Print Process, Delhi.

Contents

Acknowledgements

My earlier researches were though focused on maritime history primarily dealing with the movement of cargoes of international trade and commerce in the early modern age it helped me gradually rethink to explore the movement of ideas and people across the world. Thereafter I began to collect documents and records on Tamil migration in the various repositories. I successfully found abundant and rich documentation on Tamil labour migration overseas from the ports of the Tamil coast to the various islands/ colonies of the French and the British. Hence I started writing this new social history of the Tamils. I am very happy to state that the work is now finally completed.

In this connection I wish to thank the authorities of the Archives Nationales, Paris; Centre des Archives de Outre-Mer, Aix-en-Provence, France; National Archives of the United Kingdom, Kew; British Library, London; Mahatma Gandhi Institute, Moka, Mauritius; National Archives of Mauritius; Archives de la Reunion, Saint-Denis; National Archives of Singapore; Arkib Negara Malaysia, Kuala Lumpur; National Archives of Sri Lanka, Colombo; National Archives of India, New Delhi and Tamilnadu State Archives, Chennai, for extending their best help and warm support. I also thank Shri Amit Garg, Gyan Books, New Delhi, for publishing the book. Many unknown facts with rich statistical documentation have been provided here and so I am certain that this book would be gladly welcomed by the Tamils across the globe.

S. JEYASEELA STEPHEN
Murdoch University
Fremantle
Western Australia

Abbreviations

ADR	Archives de la Reunion, Saint-Denis
ANSOM	Archives Nationales, Section Outre-Mer, Paris
ANM	Arkib Negara Malaysia, Kuala Lumpur
BC	Board's Collection
BL	British Library, London
BPP	British Parliamentary Papers
CAOM	Centre des Archives de Outre-Mer, Aix-en-Provence
CO	Colonial Office Records
DRACEB	Department of Revenue, Agriculture and Commerce: Emigration Branch
JIAEA	Journal of the Indian Archipelago and Eastern Asia
MGI	Mahatma Gandhi Institute, Moka
MJC	Madras Judicial Consultations
MPP	Madras Public Proceedings
NAI	National Archives of India, New Delhi
NAM	National Archives of Mauritius
NAS	National Archives of Singapore
NASL	National Archives of Sri Lanka, Colombo
NAUK	National Archives of the United Kingdom, Kew
OIOC	Oriental and India Office Collection
SSFR	Straits Settlements Factory Records
SSRSC	Straits Settlements Records: Singapore Consultations
TNSA	Tamilnadu State Archives, Chennai

Chapter - 1

Introduction

People who lived in different parts of the world had migrated from one place to another owing to changing climatic conditions, in search of food and water for themselves and for the cattle which they reared. Society of the pre-historic, the historic, the ancient and the medieval times have been changing with the coming of the outsiders and the ways in which the society moved in depth is significant. Migration was part of the lives of people and in India too we find large scale internal movement of people. In ancient and medieval Indian history it has been much neglected by scholars and it is therefore important to understand the explicit regional specificities that developed over a period of time.

Migration in Tamil History and the Society down the Ages

There has been large scale movement of people in the inland from one place to another and the migrations evolved to help the people and their social life came to be changed over the long span of time. Sangam literary sources in Tamil explicitly mention the advent of the Aryans from the Himalayas. We find a place called Mullur that came into existence in the Tamil region with the coming of the Aryans.[1] It has been generally mentioned by the scholars that caste was a dominant factor in ancient Indian society and most of the writers have included the religious and cultural elements and they have largely presented a mixed bag without addressing the then functioning social system. Hence it is very necessary to bring out the regional developments in the making of particular linguistic communities and the way in which those who migrated into Tamil country and how they came to participate and function within the rubric of the local Tamil, regional and the then known the global world environment.

Man in the beginning wondered at the nature which was a surprise to him with regard to its functioning that could not be comprehended by the human mind. Therefore he began to worship nature. In course of time, humans began to offer some explanations to which they were worshipping and developed the worship of the supernatural beings. Thereafter the worship of the deities and gods emerged along the lines of religion. The rise of religions gave birth to the view that God had created the world as explained by the humans. The worship and the social relationship of the people of various sections in Tamil country are important and it is noted that Vedic rituals had come into vogue and began to be performed in the Sangam age. The three rulers of Tamil country namely Perungkilli the Chola king, Maari Venko the Chera king and Ukkira Peruvazhuthi the Pandya king had participated in a *yaagam* (yagnya) and their participation in the sacrifice and ritual had been observed by Avvaiayar the poetess who sang 'be united together'. This has been mentioned in the text of Puranaanuru.[2] In the Vedic age particularly in Rig veda, we find that there were no castes. Later we find caste distinctions that had begun to strike roots in Yajur veda. The Upanishads and Dharma sastras which came to be composed much later had then began to expand the caste distinctions. However it has been reported that castes were chiefly based on professions and occupations. The *catur varna* system had been provided by scholars only as a ground for intellectual development or expression of the early Indian society. In India, the Hindu religion and god worship had been used as tools for establishing caste system. Manu dharma saasthiram has been ascribed to BC 200 which serves a work of justification between castes and living style, system and daily life. Existence of four *varnas* had been mentioned and found only in Hinduism and just attested by Manu alone. But the *jatis* had been included in relation to religion. There is confusion as to as what is *jati* and what is religion in ancient India. Citizens and people did some jobs and they were employed. Whether these can be classified into forms such as *jatis* and castes and communities and what is the basis for such a thing is largely unknown to us.

With the migration of people from the north of Tamil country, there were two types of brahmins in Tamil region. They were called *anthanars* and *paaarpanar* in Tamil. Maduraikanchi the Tamil literary text mentions that *anthanars* sang the vedas. They also went from place to place and explained the *vedanthas*. Mullaipaatu the Tamil literary source mentions that there were Tamil brahmins who spoke Sanskrit like the Aryans. Paripaadal the Tamil literary text mentions that the *paarpanars* and *anthanars* came to bathe in river Vaigai and they just returned without bathing for some reasons.[3] We find in Tamil literary sources that *paarpanars* were employed in royal courts and they also acted as messengers.[4]

Inland Migration of the Brahmins from the North to Tamil Country

It is known that non-vedic religions like Jainism and Buddhism spread and flourished in ancient Tamil country. Later these religions declined and we find saivism and vaishnavism began to gain momentum in Tamil country during the eighth century. The migration of the Telugu speaking brahmins, displacement, homelessness, exile, loss of identity had been found mention in the inscriptions. The voluntary or forcible movement of people from their Telugu homelands into new region of Tamil country is a central historical fact of the *brahmadeya* settlements. Owing to knowledge in Vedas and sastras the brahmins who settled were richly rewarded by the rulers and they granted agricultural lands and villages. The donees of the granted land by the Pallava rulers were exempted from the payment of taxes to the state.[5]

New systems came to be adopted and followed when villages came to be donated to brahmins. A female elephant was let loose in the morning and it was allowed to move on in its own way. This was followed by the mahout concerned along with a number of officials related to revenue and administration departments. Generally the elephant after starting from a fixed point usually moved clockwise from eastern direction of the village supposed to be donated. It reached the starting point by completing its circle in the evening. The officials concerned who accompanied the trip made a note of the boundaries and marked them with stones and bushes and it has been explained in copper plate inscriptions. Practically the boundary details were needed for the revenue and administrative purposes.[6]

The Pullur plates of Nandivaraman Pallavamalla mention that lands were granted to 108 brahmins in AD. 765. We find mention of Pullur, Kudiyur, Nelli and Tekkuru the four villages situated on the banks of river Cheyyaru were clubbed together and were granted to 108 brahmins of various *gotras* and *sutras*.[7] Tandanthottam plates of Nandivarman Pallavamalla II register the lands granted to a number of brahmins in AD 789 at Nalgur situated six miles west of Kumbakonam. All brahmin *gotras* and *sutras* are here recorded who were proficient in Vedic knowledge with titles such as *chaturvedi*, *somayaji*, *trivedi*, *shadangavid* and *dasapuriya*. The neat mention of the titles such as *somayaji*, *vasantayaji*, *savadratuyaji*, *vajpeyi*, *shadgavid*, *bhatta*, *kramavita* and *chaturvedi* refer to performance of vedic sacrifices and their learning. There had been not a single brahmin donee belonged to the *vaikhanasa sutra*, the priests of Vishnu temple. These migrants had hailed from Guntur, Krishna and Nellore districts and the places mentioned include Tanukkil, Irakandoru, Irugandi, Karnjari, Pinikkiparru, Popaaru, Attamabru, Mudiparu, Viripparu, Arasaparru, Nutikaparru, Ponnambarru. We find the list that included 244 brahmin donees.[8] It is interesting to note that this Tandanthottam plates of Nandivarman record the gift of a whole village called Dayamukha mangalam to 308 Brahmins.[9] We find here the migration of brahmins of 45 *gotras* hailing from 88 villages from Telugu speaking regions of Guntur, Ongalur and Nellore to Tamil Country and they had settled under the patronage of the Pallavas.[10]

The stone inscription at Bahoor in AD 958 describes Rashtrakuta King Krishna III (AD 939–66) who had extended patronage to vaishnava brahmins (*bhattars*) through land grants known as *bhatta vritii.*[11] Brahmins, were thus, encouraged to settle in the Tamil region. Inscriptions also tell us of mixed communities in the vicinity of Pondicherry, where brahmin bridegrooms married *vaishya* brides and they were engaged in part-time weaving.[12] Thus it is known that caste feelings were not dominant and there were inter-caste marriages with the large scale inland migration of the brahmins.

Migration of Telugu brahmins in large number into Tamil country had continued even in the later period. The Karandhai plates of Rajendra Chola I (1012-44) refer to lands and villages given to 1083 brahmins in AD 1020. Of which 775 brahmin donees were migrants from Andhra. Majority of them belong to *apastambha sutra* and 54 to *baudhayana.* The brahmins who are stated here hailed from places with Tamil names belonged to mostly sutras other than *apstambha*, i.e., *asvalayana*, *drahyayuna*, *satyashadha*, *jaimini* etc. This proves that brahmins had moved in a group belonging to particular combination of *gotra/sutra* other than *apastambha* and they had migrated and settled.[13] Rajendra Chola established Tirubhuvanamaadevi Chaturvedimangalam and it was made over to 108 brahmins.[14] Sadayavarman Sundra Pandya I formed a brahmin village in Chidambaram area and 300 *velis* of land was apportioned among 121 brahmins. The village also made provision for settling the *vellalars* (agriculturalists) and plots of land were allotted to various professionals such as *vaidyars* (physicians) *karnam* (accountant) *thachchars* (carpenters) *kollars* (blacksmith) *uvachar* (drummer) *naavidhar* (barber) *kurumban* (potter) *padai kaaval* (watchman) and *vettiyan* (village servant).[15]

Free gifts of lands and villages were continued to be made to brahmins. The brahmins from Tamil country had also migrated to Nirgunda situated in Kogali area in Karnataka in 1087. It was then numerous *brahmadeya* villages had come to be created in the present-day Chennapatna taluk of Bangalore district.[16] It happened so following the Chola conquests and the rulers were fully convinced to the point of the economic interests of the Tamil émigrés. Thus the brahmins were migrating from one place to another in search of income and livelihood. Brahmins had also migrated en masse owing to severe religious conflicts that broke out in the medieval period. Jainism and Buddhism when declined brahmins in large number came to Tamil country and settled down.

Inscriptions in Tamil country mention brahmins as *ayyan* as late as in AD 1263.[17] They were given lands as donations and these were called *brahmadeyas*. In the Pudukottai region some places such as Chittur, Tiruvengaivasal, Tiruvilangudi, Peravur, Kiranur, Kappukud and Kadavambatti developed and they were important brahmadeya settlements.[18] It has been reported that between the fifth century and fifteenth century there were 165 *brahmadeyas* in Thondaimandalam, 180 *brahmadeyas* in nadunaadu (South Arcot area) and Cholanaadu and 205 *brahmadeyas* in Pandiyanaadu.[19] The rulers of Telugu country patronized Buddhism and so Nagarjunakonda and Amaravati became prominent centres. Therefore the migration of brahmins had happened from the Telugu region on a large scale and they came to settle in Tamil country.[20]

The Resistance Put-up by the Non-Brahmins for the Growth and Development of the Brahmin Settlements in Tamil Country

Rulers of Tamil country encouraged the brahmins who migrated. They did so without awarding any privileges and concessions to the natives. They also wished and encouraged the non-brahmins to live within the settlements of the brahmins. This is noted while founding of a new village for the brahmins. The inscription mentions that a temple was there with a tank and the brahmins were given right to walk to the tank to conduct their religious rituals. The following *panimakkal* (i.e., people of services) were established in the village which included teachers of sutras, physicians, village accountant, drummer, potter, blacksmith, carpenter, goldsmith, barber, washermen, watchmen and village servant. Thus there were fourteen castes found mention in the record and each group had a separate living quarters.[21] Though brahmins held lands in the *brahmadeyas* they did not engage themselves directly in the cultivation of land but they depended on peasants, tenants and agricultural labourers. Hence there were two distinct communities emerged such as the landholders and cultivators in the *brahmadeya* villages.[22]

The brahmin settlements in Tamil were called *brahmanacheri*. The *shanars* (toddy tappers) were not allowed to live there. Rulers granted lands to Brahmins and marked the boundaries. Maravarman Sundara Pandya II (AD.1216-1244) granted lands to 224 *chatur vedi bhattars* (vaishanava Brahmins) in 1224 in Tirunelveli.[23]

Counteraction had been exercised by the *vellalars* against the creation of *brahmadeyas* as early as in the eighth century. The creation of new *brahmadeya* settlements amidst the *vellanvagai* villages (cultivators' villages) caused problems and it is learnt from the Dalavypuram copper plate.[24] In the Velvikudi plates it is mentioned that the Velvikudi village once granted had been taken back.[25] The Pandya inscriptions of the eighth and ninth centuries thus speak of the loss of such lands and also encroachment. Later we find inscriptions being engraved against the misappropriation of lands granted to brahmins and also protection of the brahmins and their properties besides extolling of the merits of protection being recorded in the land grant charters. Noboru Karashima opines that it was at that time the villages donated to brahmins began to function by chiefly integrating and controlling the surrounding non-*brahmadeya* villages.[26]

Raja Raja Chola I gave an order implicitly that the lands of the non-*brahmadeya* landholders within the *brahmadeya* villages should be sold away.[27] Pandya king Paranthaka Vira Narayana refers to a gift of lands to twelve brahmins. Subsequently another grant of *brahmadeya* is noticed and it was made by the Pandya king. In the course of time, a non-brahmin who was affected seriously (because of the land grant) came to encroach upon the *brahmadeya* land. He claimed that the land was his own. One of the brahmins therefore appealed the matter to the king through an officer of the ruler. The king examined the case and gave a fresh judgment by restoring the land to its original donee. In this case the confidential secretary of the king was made a witness to the case.[28] Evidences suggest that the numerous grants of *brahmadeya* lands were opposed by the people for they were affected. It was chiefly so because while establishing a *brahmadeya*, an existing institution's proprietary and administrative rights over unused land were relinquished in favour of the brahmin donees. Further attempts were made also and steps were initiated largely towards curbing the growth of *brahmadeyas* by non-brahmins in Tamil country. It was because the brahmins had no talents except with their skill reciting the Vedas. The local people felt that the migrant brahmins were unable to contribute substantially towards the growth of economy.

Social Life of the Brahmins

Lands granted to brahmins in Tamil were called *agarapattru*.[29] The brahmins gave the lands for cultivation to the farmers and received paddy in kind. In the event of eventualities when crops failed owing to failure of monsoon, the brahmins compelled the farmers to supply the grain. They also levied fines on the peasants and cultivators. In AD 1118 the *mahasabha* of Sri Rajadhiraja Chaturvedimangalam a *brahmadeya* in Suthamalli *valanadu* resolved to collect twice the amount of tax from the defaulters.[30] In 1123 the *mahasabaha* of Kavantantalam a *brahmadeya* in Thondaimandalam received 20 *kasus* as land tax from an individual.[31] As early as in AD 1150 Srivaishnava brahmins had requested the ruler to exempt them from payment of land taxes. The ruler had also accepted their request and granted exemption.[32] An inscription of Kailasanatha temple at Mannargudi in Thanjavur region in AD 1169 mentions that the *perungudigal* (peasants) were supposed to pay the tax arrears called *kadamai* in the name of brahmins. It had been reported also that for the non-payment of tax arrears, the state officials should not capture the brahmins and throw them in custody or jail.[33]

Brahmins paid a poll tax called *perkadmai* as mentioned in the records.[34] They saw to that they were not levied any other taxes by the rulers, while the other castes like weavers, shepherds, smiths and other craftsmen besides *chetti* merchants continued to pay taxes. It had been found mention that the brahmins at Tirukachchur in Chingleput area revolted against the state government in AD 1289 and so they were captured and imprisoned in jail.[35] *Thandam* (fines) were imposed upon the Siva brahmanas of Uthiramerur and they had paid.[36]

The Siva brahmanas and the Vaishnava brahmanas lived separately in different areas in the various settlements and also adopted different habits and customs. There was no marriage conducted between these two groups.[37] Amongst the vaishnava brahmanas there were also two other sects called the *vadakali* (the northern) and the *thenkalai* (the southern).[38] A group of brahmins were called *othuvaars* and they chanted the mantras and made their livelihood. These men were also employed in the vedic schools where they taught the brahmin students Sanskrit language, vedanta and other Hindu religious subjects.[39] Rulers made liberal grants to these vedic schools and they were called *vidya bhogam* and thereby helped those brahmins employed in the vedic schools.[40] There functioned a vedic school at Kanchipuram.[41] Ennaiyiram village had another vedic school attached to the temple. It had 350 students and out of which 230 students were only involved in Vedic studies. It had 11 teachers too.[42] Similar to this we find another school that functioned at Tirubhuvanai near Pondicherry in AD 1048 and it was attached to the local temple of Varadaraja Perumal.[43] Liberal grants were made and adequate steps were taken by the rulers to look after the welfare of the students and the school. The brahmin population had enormously increased over the period of time and we find from the inscription of Kanyakumari that during the rule of Vira Rajendra Chola (the third son of Rajendra Chola) there were 40,000 brahmins in Tamil country who were said to be masters in the Vedas and received plenty of gifts of land and had settled in many *brahmadeya* villages.[44]

In this age numerous Saiva agamas and the Vaishnava agamas were composed and they described the conduct of rituals and worship in the temples. Further the celebration of various festivals and feasts were also enumerated. In addition to the temples, we find also the madams (religious mutts) that had sprang up.[45] Religious instruction and free food had been provided here besides rendering some medical services to the people. We find in the inscriptions wherein numerous grants in cash and kind were made over to these mutts.[46] In several mutts *saraswati bhandaram* (libraries) had functioned where palm leaf manuscripts were prepared and preserved.[47]

Those brahmins associated with temple rituals and worship were called *devakanmis*. In the beginning when Buddhism and Jainism were popular the Brahmins did not receive the adequate and generous support. As a result the brahmin priests suffered very much to sustain their own lives and families.[48] Brahmins who were employed in temple service at that time had devised a plan so as to receive food daily from the temples. In many cases, special types of food were prepared on feast and festival days and also on *amaavaasai* (no moon days) and they were offered to the deities and also consumed by the brahmins besides offering the same food which was called *prasaadam* (sacrificial food) to the devotees who visited.[49] We find abundant details regarding the preparation of food besides *laddu* and other sweets in the temple kitchens.[50] The food prepared and supplied developed in such a fashion later which included cooked rice, and side-dishes prepared out of 5 types of vegetables. It was consumed by the Brahmins besides supply of curd, ghee, betel leaves and areca nuts.[51] Later we find in records that paddy was supplied annually to the brahmins employed in temples for their maintenance besides dress.[52]

There arose stiff competition among the brahmin priests in the temples over a period of time. It is reported that the priests in the temple of Vidyarayapuram at Thittagudi in Cuddalore area in AD 1399 came to an amicable settlement among themselves bringing to an end a long standing dispute about the proportionate shares of performing worship that each of them were entitled to in the temple.[53] In Tirupati there were 24 brahmins attached to the Tiruvengadam temple and they were employed there for reciting the Vedas as late as in AD 1433.[54] Brahmin priests in the temple had also received fruits as gifts as found in inscriptions.[55] Many rulers and individuals contributed large sums of money to the temple. The amount realized was mainly allotted for preparation and supply of food. Aa. Sivasubramanian opines that the arrangements made for the supply of food in the temple and the investments had not yielded profitable return. Hence it had not at all helped for the noble cause of social development.[56] Aa. Sivasubramanian in fact had failed to point out that the scheme was just devised in such a way to help and feed the brahmins alone. The moral justification offered by the brahmins at that time was that the financial help extended to offer the food would bring spiritual gain and benefit in the next birth.

Donations were made by the kings on festivals too. Several gifts were also made by the affluent merchant guilds. The traders and other individual donors who were wealthy also contributed to the temples. The forms of wealth of the temple largely included plots of land in the villages, moveable property, gold and other jewels, gifts of money, cattle and grain. As the kings had made large donations and liberal grants to the temple it was found necessary to have a careful watch over the temple properties. Hence arrangements were made to inspect the accounts by appointing officials and auditors.[57] In AD 992 an officer had scrutinized the account of the temple at Tiruvallam. He had detected the misappropriation of lands by the Siva brahamans of the temple and levied a compensatory fine of 74 *kalangu* of gold.[58] Similarly the lands of an individual who held accountancy rights of several temples were confiscated in AD 1224 because he committed acts of treason against god and king by misappropriating the temple property.[59] Further we find a brahmin misappropriating the property of the temple and he was ordered by the king to be punished by the royal officials.[60]

In AD 1152 the temple priests of Panthananallur stole the gold kept for making jewels at the treasury of the temple. When it was detected their *puja* rights were taken back. It was sold to other brahmins and the amount realized was 180 *kasus*. It was ordered that *puja* rights in the near future should not be given to those who committed theft or to those of their generations.[61] Again in a case we find confiscation of property of individuals in AD 1184 for the embezzlement of temple properties.[62] Hence it is learnt that these brahmin priests would have suffered without proper employment and must have found difficult to run the families.

In AD 1194 the manger of temple at Govindaputtur had fraudulently taken away the temple funds. Hence his property was confiscated and his house was demolished and over the remains of it, a temple was built.[63] In AD 1244 Pillai Yadvarayar had conducted an inquiry and he found that an individual who held the account rights of several temples had misappropriated the paddy stored in the temple godowns and also he had also embezzled a portion of the money deposited in the temple treasuries.[64] In AD 1374 the trustees of Tirukalukundram temple had to confiscate and sell the properties of a temple functionary who by breaking the strong-room of Tirukalukunramudaiyar temple stole a sum of 150 *pon*.[65] Thus many brahmins who were employed in the temples had led high immoral life.

In AD 1099 the utensils kept and used for the *puja* in the temple and the ornaments worn by the deity were found missing and it was learnt that they were stolen by the brahmin priests. The value of the stolen articles was estimated to 240 *kasus*. When the matter was brought to the kind notice of the ruler, he immediately ordered that the amount should be recovered and paid back to the temple. One of the temple priests had expressed his inability to pay the sum and he agreed to give in compensation to lose the *puja* rights. Hence the amount was realized through the method of auction.[66] In AD 1184 utensils belonging to the temple and the ornaments worn by the deity were stolen by the Brahmins. Hence the land and sites belonged to the brahmins were sold in auction and the proceeds were paid into the treasury.[67] In AD 1213 the house of a brahmin who had robbed the *thirupattam* (head ornament) of the deity was confiscated.[68] It is reported that the siva brahmanas who committed theft in the temple were fined and they paid 420 kasus.[69] In AD 1289 brahmins had stolen the objects belonging to a temple.[70] In some brahmin cases it is reported that brahmin family as a whole was engaged in thefts. In AD 1289 a brahmin, his wife and his daughter-in-law were involved and they had indulged at various intervals in stealing the temple objects, vessels, and jewels.[71] The reason for such a theft must be either poverty that prevailed or avarice and greediness.

Temple properties were found often misused by the brahmins and they have been also noted down in the records. In AD 1225 at Tirunagesvaram two brahmin brothers and another person had embezzled temple property and they took the costly clothes used by god for their own use. They had also used the bricks meant for the use of the temple by misappropriating the bricks for their own building construction.[72] In AD 1225 at Thiruvarangam the temple priests and officers of the management had collided with *ottars* (stone workers) and misappropriated the temple property. When detected the brahmins were not punished but an order was passed that they should not continue to hold the office in the temple. They were only banned in the near future from being employed in the temple.[73] However, the *ottars* were severely punished. Thus unjust legal procedures were then followed and this practice had allowed the brahmins to continue to do criminal activities.

In AD 1255 at Kudumiyanmalai some of the brahmin priests had stolen cash, jewels and ornaments belonging to the temple. A stone sculptor was also involved in the act along with the brahmin priests and he received his share to a sum of 60 *pon*. During the inquiry conducted all those who stole did not accept the crime. Hence hot red iron was asked to be taken in their hands to prove that they did not steal. It was at that time the culprits came to accept the crime and offence. As a result they had to pay the fine imposed.[74] A record from Pudukottai refers to a meeting of the inhabitants of the locality and stated that the *pujas* in the temple of Tirunalakkunra Mudaiya Nayanar had been stopped when cash and jewels of temple were stolen. During an inquiry one of the brahmins confessed his crime and he admitted that a portion of lost cash was shared by him with a carpenter. The other priests of the temple denied all knowledge of the lost cash and properties. Therefore these priests were ordered to take the red hot ploughshare in their hands. When they did so and after having burnt they confessed their guilt.[75] Thus it is found that many brahmin priests were found to be liars and thieves and they led a life scandalous.

During the rule of Sadayavarman Sundara Pandya in the thirteenth century Vaamana Bhattar was employed as one of the temple officers of Thirukottiyur Madhavan temple. After finishing his job as usual in the temple having closed the temple gates, he was returning through the east car street and at that time he was killed by Sathyanaavan and his group of men. After a few days, the relatives of Vaamana Bhattar in retaliation to the death had planned and killed Sathyanaavan.[76] Thus we find the attitude of vengeance prevalent among the brahmins. In an another instance it is reported that a person was tied to the leg of a buffalo and he was dragged for having murdered a brahmin.[77] Thus brahmins had taken the law into their own hands. It is not known clearly from records why the brahmins were killed and what were the actual reasons. However, the atrocities committed by the brahmins were not tolerated by the rulers. In one instance we find that Kulotunga Chola II (AD 113-1150) had awarded and executed the capital punishment to a brahmin. The Thiruvidaimarudur Puranam records this event.[78]

High corruption activities had begun to play its own part as the temple workers were increasingly appointed in service. The officials including the *karanikkar*, *kadaikuttar* and others were admonished by king Devaraya II (AD 1425-46) for he passed a royal order banning them from demanding any commission from those people who supplied the articles required for use in the temple.[79]

Brahmins continued to lead lives of scandal as found in records. There was a brahmin by name Avani Settu who lived in the brahmin settlement of Uthipakkam alias Aadhinaayaga Chaturvedimangalam in AD 1289. His five sons (Atkondavallan, Paambanaiyan, Malavaykon, Varadhan and Salavani) had often indulged in scolding and abusing the brahmin girls and women of the locality in filthy language. In spite of the warnings issued they were found to be incorrigible. Hence all the five sons of Avani Settu were caught and tied to a pillar. They were beaten so severely and punished for the misdeed.[80]

Inscriptions record numerous incidents of immoral behaviour and illegal contacts between the brahmins and *devaradiyals* of the temples. An inscription of AD 1239 at Sivapuram registers immoral behaviour of two Siva brahmanas with *devaradiayals*.[81] Gross mismanagement on the part of a brahmin manager of the temple at Tirupattur had been coupled with misconduct with a brahmin widow who came from a distant place and settled there. The assembly of Tirupattur therefore in AD 1291 lodged a complaint to Maravarman Kulasekhara Pandya the ruler. We are unable to know the action taken by the king and his judgment delivered since the details inscribed at the end of the epigraph had been lost.[82] The Siva brahmanas in a temple had stolen the jewels of the temples and they gave it to the concubine which they admitted on inquiry.[83] We find as late as in the seventeenth century that a brahmin in the temple at Malayadipatti was found in amorous ways with Vadula Mangai a *devaradiyal*. This woman was a good dancer and she was employed later in the royal court of Avudiya Thevan at Puchchikudi. When the chieftain learnt the news of her immoral conduct with the brahmin he was so angry. Hence he killed both of them.[84]

During the expansion and rule of the Vijayanagra kings into Tamil country many brahmins who spoke Kannada and Telugu had migrated. It was at that time marriages with Tamil Brahmins had become the need of the hour. An order issued by king Devaraya II in 1426 is an important and note worthy of mention here. It states that the brahmins of Padaividu *rajya* comprising of the various linguistic communities of Kannada, Telugu and Tamil of all *gotras*, *sutras* and *sakhas* should conduct marriages as simple *kanyaadan* without bridegroom's family giving money (dowry) to the bride's family. If as against this royal order, money was exchanged for bride, it would occur royal punishment. It would also be considered against the brahmanical norms.[85] This clearly points out the fact that the dowry system at that time came to be changed and a new practice had come into vogue. It also explains the non-availability of the brahmin brides when compared to the availability of the brahmin bridegrooms. With the coming of the rule of the Marathas in Thanjavur we find also many maharatta brahmins had come in large number and they settled in Tamil country. It may be said that with the advent of the brahmins Sanskrit language had come to be spread in Tamil country but no new technological innovation were introduced in Tamil society.

Migration of the Telugu and Kannada Weavers to Tamil Country and the Patronage Extended by the Medieval Rulers and the People

Pattu saliyars and padma saliyars (thenkalai vaishnavites) were Telugu speaking weavers who had migrated to Tamil country and did weaving as early as in the ninth century.[86] They had settled at Kanchipuram under the patronage of the Pallava rulers and spread as far Cheranmahadevi in Pandyamandalam and wove silk cloth and produced other high varieties of cloth.[87] They conducted also trade in textiles and so the rulers levied heavy professional taxes on them. As a result they suffered and showed their protest and resistance by migrating to other places. It had been reported that the *saliyars* at Tiruvaamathur when migrated owing to tax burden the local officials had appealed to them to return.[88]

Maravarman Vira Pandya had encouraged the *saliyars* to settle at Chidambaram and he granted plots of land to build their own settlement.[89] During the rule of Kulotunga Chola III (1178-1218) the *saliyars* left Chidambaram owing to tax burden.[90] Samburvaraya rulers in the fourteenth century encouraged the *saliyars* to come and settle at Tirukachchiyur and conduct weaving.[91] *Saliyars* lived at Paththamadai near Tirunelveli and produced high quality cloth.[92] Thus migration of the *saliyars* from Telugu country took place in the medieval period and they were spread all over Tamil country. Later in the early modern age *saliyars* also migrated from Mattewade, Bapatla, Chirala, Warangal and Nellore to Madras (Chennaipattinam) and lived under the patronage of the English East India Company.[93]

Kannada speaking weavers called *devangars* had migrated to Thiruvaanaikaaval in Tamil country under the patronage extended by the Hoysala rulers as early as in AD 1339.[94] Later we find their settlements had spread at Kapisthalam, Thiruvaamathur, Anniyur and Villiyanallur during the sixteenth century.[95] With the arrival of these weavers and dyers we find new textile weaving and dyeing technology had come to be introduced.[96] The rulers and the state benefitted very much because of the increased revenue. Thus long term benefits were derived and there was no resistance put up by the Tamils for the advent of the Telugu and Kannada speaking weavers. There had been also no differences of opinion or commercial rivalry and competition or ill feelings and bitter experience or conflicts reported amongst them.

During the rule of the Sultanates of Delhi Allauddin Khilji sent his general Malik Kafur to Tamil country. This army reached Madurai on 13 April 1311 and it left the place on 25 April 1311 with its booty. The army had looted along the route it passed through and the local people who suffered had migrated to other places called *anginaan pugalidam* (safe place for those who are afraid) as found mention in the numerous Tamil inscriptions.[97] Weavers and merchants who were affected quickly moved over to these *anginaan pugalidam* temporarily. However it took long time to return to their original homes. We find the help and assistance rendered to these migrants by the Samburvaraya rulers between AD 1335 and 1380.[98]

Migration of the Merchants and the Development of Overseas Trade

The overseas commercial contacts developed between the Mediterranean, the Red Sea region and Tamil country is well known to us. Iravadam Mahadevan had proposed that the Indus valley civilization was the result of the migrated Tamils. His researches help us to prove that the Indus valley culture was of Dravidian origin. In the medieval period Tamil traders sailed across the oceans and conducted trade with various parts of South Asia. The merchant trading guilds functioned such as *manigrammam*, *thisai ayiraththu ainnurruvar* known as Ayyavole sometimes prefixed with the term *nanadesi* besides *viravanchiyar* and *anjuvannam* guilds were engaged in trade and commerce and carried out extensive shipping and it enabled growth of trade both locally and overseas. We find their presence in South East Asia from the numerous Tamil inscriptions.[99] Many families of the *chettiyars*, *mudaliars* and *marakkayars* had come to travel and they settled in various parts of South East Asia.[100] *Komuti chettis*, *Beri chettis* and *Kavari chettis* too migrated from Andhra and settled down at the various European port settlements on the Tamil coast during the seventeenth and eighteenth centuries. The wealthy business families of Malayya, Chinnaana, Beri Thimmanna, Kasi Veeranna, Venkatadri, Chekka Serappa, Sunku Rama, Sunku Muthu Rama and Sunku Seshachala migrated to Tamil country invested huge amount of funds and earned handsome profits.[101]

After the advent of the Portuguese, Dutch, Danes, French and the English on the Tamil coast we find the overseas trade had developed in an unprecedented manner. Contacts between various places in Europe and Tamil country were established while a few Tamils had travelled and sailed to Europe in ships. Three Tamils had reached Lisbon and they had helped in the printing works of the first Tamil book titled *cartilha* which got printed on 2 February 1554 in Portugal.[102] Timothy Kuttiyan sailed from Tranquebar in 1711 and Peter Malayappan in 1715 and they reached Copenhagen in Denmark and Halle in Germany.[103] Manuel Jagan in 1707 and Nayniyappa Pillai in 1718 had sailed from Pondicherry and reached Paris in France.[104] However Tamils on a large scale had migrated overseas in the age of colonial development and expansion. Hence the present book aims to study the life of the Tamils who migrated overseas across the world and explores their social life.

Design of the Study

Chapter one introduces the subject proper by analyzing the inland migration of people from various parts of India into Tamil country. It also traces the overseas trade and temporary migration of merchants and businessmen in the medieval period. The Europeans sought to achieve the dominance on land during the eighteenth century that they had been unable to achieve in the earlier two centuries. The process was facilitated by the progressive weakening of Tamil kingdoms unable to compete with Western military superiority. The Tamil labour migration across geographical spaces and localities developed at that time and a wide range of cover has been undertaken with a diverse range of conceptual tools and terminologies. The focus of the crossroads of Tamil society had been therefore aimed at a comparative study of Tamil migration flows across the oceans during French and British colonial rule. In what way did these labour flows impact the society in the long-term? And what kind of relationship came to be evolved between the Europeans and the Tamil communities across time and space? These are some of the questions addressed in the chapters when modern industrial capitalism and the consequent colonization of Asia, Africa, the Caribbean and other parts of the world by the British and the French triggered a massive mobilization of Tamil agrarian communities and various professionals of several castes across these diverse geographical localities. The growing demand for raw materials and other tropical agricultural products in the West had led to the establishment of large-scale plantations using European capital for the production of export commodities such as sugar and coffee, for which a labour force was mobilized from different districts of Tamil country to the overseas colonies of the French in Mauritius, Reunion and the French West Indies besides the British Empire in Mauritius, Ceylon and Malaya. The evolution of the Tamil society aboard or overseas is important and we find growth and development after being transported slaves and free workers and later as skilled and unskilled workers. Those people migrated en masse across the globe had been promoted by the colonial age and so we study the convoy of passengers and emigrants.

Chapter two examines in depth the migration of Tamils from Pondicherry to Mauritius and Reunion Islands under the banner of the French East India Company from 1729 to 1883. It is noticed that free labour migration developed in the beginning and how the sailors were made responsible ready for enlisting workers. We find the migration of coolie labourers later and the labour system developed leading into signing contracts and it ensured the return voyages that were successfully conducted. Over a period of time two thirds of the migrants preferred to stay in Mauritius and also they were compelled to remain being further indentured. Large scale immigration statistics of coolies from Pondicherry and Karaikal to Reunion have been found for the period from 1841 to 1883. The return of coolies to Pondicherry had been also gleaned from the records from 1849 to 1883. It is argued that the coolie system emerged was a mixture of various labour systems and it stood somewhere between slavery and free labour and the French were the pioneers on the Tamil Coast in this regard. The social and religious practices of Tamil Hindus, Muslims and Christians who lived in Mauritius had been explored.

Chapter three is directed towards the migration of Tamil indentured labour from Pondicherry and Karaikal to French West Indies and their life style in the sugar plantations between 1851 and 1879. The abolition of slavery in the West Indies necessitated the need for labour from French

India. Therefore the emigration society of Pondicherry was founded in 1851 and two agencies were created for recruiting coolies while one had functioned at Pondicherry and the other at Karaikal. As the French being the pioneers on the Tamil coast the British in Madras tried to learn the matters especially the labour recruitment method and transport by deputing persons from Madras to Pondicherry. The facts collected were informed to the authorities in London. It was found that *maistries* (chiefs) were approached and they were asked to recruit labourers for a group of coolies who boarded the French ships. The cost of immigration was fixed and contractual arrangements were executed for a period of three years. The migration rose chiefly owing to the pressure of demand from the French planters in Guiana, Martinique and Guadeloupe islands. It was reported that people from British Indian territory were largely recruited and sent to French ports. The *maistries* functioned as brokers and they were approved by the French government. The tedious voyage of 3 to 4 months led to the high rate of deaths in the ships. A surgeon was appointed on board to look after and help the coolie migrants who fell ill and became very sick. The French authorities sent books printed in Pondicherry to French Guiana and it was found useful both for the French planters to know Tamil and for the Tamil children of the coolies to learn French at school. It is argued that trans-Atlantic slavery in the past had an impact and it influenced the Tamil migration in the later period. Against this backdrop the migration of Tamils of various castes to French West Indies had been situated. Those who migrated had included mainly agricultural workers besides masons, shepherds, weavers and others. The statistical records show how coolies had also returned from French West Indies to Tamil country between 1855 and 1882.

Chapter four deals with immigration of Tamils from Madras under the British between 1829 and 1890 and particularly the indentured labourers recruited for Mauritius following the French footsteps. Since slavery was abolished in British India in 1843 and coolies were recruited and sent to Mauritius from Madras and Pondicherry. Madras became the main centre of emigration to Mauritius under English after 1864. Coolies from Thanjavur, Tiruchirapalli and South Arcot districts were recruited and migrated at first and mostly they were cultivators recruited for five years on a salary of 5 rupees per month besides allowances and clothes. They were paid in advance the wages of three months. The chapter documents well the four kinds of systems that were under operation. We find the bounty system of labour recruitment in the beginning which was prevalent till 1843. The contingent system was introduced in 1844 wherein fixed quota of immigrants had to be brought to Mauritius monthly and strict selections in quality of labourers were emphasized. It was at that point of time the wages of the coolies paid had been increased to 7 rupees in 1842 as an additional inducement. Later the system of free man entry as a labourer was encouraged and it introduced the method whereby the free man was at liberty to execute with the planters in Mauritius a contract after arrival in Mauritius in 1852. Over a period of time, a change in the labour policy was felt as the need of the hour and in 1853 the free return passage to coolies got abolished. Thus finally the contingent system was again replaced by a contract system in Mauritius in 1854 and thereafter recruitment of coolies became strict. Migration developed with coolie migrants largely recruited from Madras and Chingleput districts at first. Later it was followed by large scale coolie recruits from Thanjavur and Tiruchirapalli regions. Thus free labour migration came to be abolished and a labourer had to sign a contract in Madras itself. Many contractors came to be appointed in 1859 by the British in the labour recruitment process in Madras. The end of the sugar boom in Mauritius between 1860 and 1880 saw the decline of Tamil migration. Though the wages of the coolies had been increased to 9 rupees as an encouragement for migration and agreed to be paid in the contracts to be signed in 1865, it has been reported that there was no labourer coming forward to set sail in ships bound for Mauritius. Most of the labourers preferred to be employed in railways and also at the plantations developed newly in the Nilgiris. Another important reason was also that the working conditions for the coolies were bad in Mauritius by 1868. The British in Madras had poured out licences to 72 labour recruiters to obtain coolies for Mauritius by 1890-91 but it was difficult and hard to find labourers for migration. Those coolies who worked very hard had saved money as found in records and they had improved their status and acquired even properties in Mauritius. The social life of the Tamils in Mauritius had been thus vividly portrayed.

Chapter five deals with the migration of Tamils to Ceylon under the aegis of British rule from 1828 to 1880. The government of Ceylon had begun to enter into direct contact with *maistries* in 1818 who acted as an agency to supply labour on contract in Tamil country. Recruitment of labourers and migration of people did not pick up any speed as desired by the British. Therefore ten years later (in 1828) the government of Ceylon took bold steps to recruit labourers directly in Tamil country. Even this was highly unsuccessful for the British could bring only 150 free labourers. These workers were not at all subjected to any control of the government. A systematic recruitment of Tamil labourers to Ceylon could develop only after 1839 and people migrated to work for a year in the coffee plantations and they returned on expiry of the period. An ordinance was passed in 1842 binding the labourers in the existing system by preventing free labour migration to Ceylon. The labourers had to compulsorily sign a contract and the law enacted gave the planters in Ceylon to take criminal action against those who violated the provisions. By 1844 the planters in Ceylon sent a *kangaani* (an overseer) from Ceylon to recruit labourers in Tamil country and the system widely came into vogue by 1847. As the migration of Tamil labourers increased the British Crown introduced a new system of official control in 1862. Migration thereafter to Ceylon came to be developed only through the two sea ports of Tuticorin and Rameswaram on the Tamil coast. Coolies were recruited in the Tamil southern hinterland were brought and assembled at a camp which was setup at Thattapaarai for labour migrants who sailed from the port of Tuticorin. Similarly coolies recruited in the hinterland in the north were brought to the camp at Mandapam for those who sailed from Rameswaram. Their travel documents and contract deeds were examined and other things were verified. With the increase in the number of coolies transported, regular service of steam ships was proposed in 1863 than transporting coolies in the ferries operated by the British government. The proposal was not welcomed and a new ordinance was passed in 1865 which allowed punishment to the labourers for neglect of duty and misconduct in service leading to criminal prosecution. Coolie labourer migration from Tamil country to Ceylon thrived on and had been on increase between 1867 and 1883 and it coincided with the famine years such as that of 1876 and 1878. Thus less control and power exercised in British India had allowed the labourers to migrate to Ceylon and there was no also strict and rigid system adopted in British Ceylon which had facilitated large scale Tamil migration. The Government of Ceylon became involved in immigrant labour policy only in 1880 through the enactment of medical wants ordinance. As a result Tamil migration till that period flourished and people of Tirunelveli coast had mainly migrated to Ceylon as per statistics.

Chapter six traces the waves of Tamil migration to Malaya between 1786 and 1878. Tamil Muslim merchants from Porto Novo and Pulicat largely traded had settled in Penang by 1786. They also returned to Tamil coast annually and it happened till 1794. After the acquisition of Penang by the English East India Company Tamil Hindus arrived since 1801 and they built a Murugan temple and the English Company gave land in George Town. Convicts from Tamil country were sent to Penang to alleviate labour shortage. These Tamil convicts filed petitions for release and return to Tamil country and the life of the exiled convicts and till their return to Tamil country in 1825 is described. The coolie recruitment and migration from Karaikal, Nagore, Nagapattinam and Madras came to develop since 1849. The number had swelled from time to time between 1850 and 1862. The crowded sailings from Nagapattinam to Penang became a major concern of the sub-collector Thanjavur district. Therefore he took bold steps to prevent especially kidnapping and transporting. He was also apprehensive that fraudulent practices had been followed and on enquiry it was found that many persons had not signed contracts at all but they produced details of their parents, uncles and guardians in Malaya and so they had boarded the ship. As the migration to Malaya had not been very properly checked through legislation by the British, the Indian Immigrants Protection Ordinance was passed in 1876 to regulate the migration and at that time the salary and the working hours of the migrants were fixed. Besides Penang, Tamils also migrated to Singapore. On founding Singapore in 1809 by Sir Stamford Raffles many Tamil Hindus and Muslims migrated and these migrants had their own shops and establishments in Singapore. Ships from Tamil Coast came and went to Singapore and Tamil migrants continued to participate in the economic activity of the island. By 1849 we notice Tamil labourers made up around 40% of the total population who were employed in Singapore. Muslims were said to be syces and owned carriages. Many Tamils worked as office peons, translators and clerks in the courts. The unskilled Tamil workers were employed as salesman in shops. Temples and mosques came to be built and the migrants had celebrated the Hindu and Muslim festivals as in Tamil country.

Chapter seven dwells on conclusions based on the above said chapters. We know that the history of the colonised world has been mainly narrated, from the deck of the ship, the ramparts of the fortress, and the high gallery of the trading factories. However, with the arrival of postcolonial studies, colonial history had lost much of its importance but concentration on the local and regional histories of the indigenous peoples in the colonies and on the pernicious effects of colonial rule had not been explored and covered. Since the 1990s historians in the West had begun to look for new ways to write imperial histories and this had to face with the changing character of their home societies. While some had started to question the foundations of the national histories, it is important to underline the significance of local and regional histories without which it is hardly possible to do anything.

Learning about local and regional history of the Tamils and more in particular the society is never a one-way process. Knowing about the past through issues that concern us in the present is also about learning the present in the light of the past. The vision of history is very broad and new and it never remained narrow. Doing history in India has been varied and more particularly ruminating on social traditions. The Tamil middle and low class, the struggle for recognition, the moral and grammar of social conflicts had been an ongoing process from medieval to modern times. The very ideas of medieval Tamil society and the social aspects fundamental to the discipline of history and sociology in the modern age have changed in the way Tamil people connected with each other in caste, religion, identity and place. How had social history equipped itself to understand the shifts from ancient to medieval and from pre-modern to modern is understood largely from jati to caste. It is not always important to note to which division a particular caste belonged. Its affiliation differed between localities, allegiances had switched over and castes also claimed neutrality. However, historical and sociological imagination could enable innovation and newness as researchers could make sense of the rapidly altering worlds the Tamil society. The book brings together research in a new and unusual site of the Tamils to present a historical portrait that bypasses the dominant categories of caste, religion etc., through which Tamil country has been historically known and represented though it is unavoidable totally. The contexts featured in the early modern age are diverse and unique and so we present the study of labourers. The journeys challenge and push the boundaries of the discipline of history and provoke a re-images of Tamils and social history.

Notes

1. Avvai Duraisamy Pillai, ed., *Pathirttupaththu*, 2nd ed., South India Saiva Siddhantha Pathippu Kazhagam, Tirunelveli, 1955, song no.11; A. Narayana Swamy Aiyar, ed., *Nattrinai*, South India Saiva Siddhantha Pathippu Kazhagam, Tirunelveli, 1976, see, Marutham 170.
2. *Puranaanuru*, ed., Swaminatha Aiyar, Madras, 1971, song 367.
3. *Paripaadal*, ed., P.V. Somasundaranar, 4th edn., Tirunelveli,1956, 2: 57-63; *Madurai Kanchi,* ed., U.V. Swaminatha Ayyar, Madras, 1974, lines 655-56; see also, Mullaipaattu, 64-66.
4. *Puranaanuru*, song 305:1-6.
5. P. Shamugam, 'Brahmadeyas in the Pallava Country', in S. Rajagopal, ed., *Kaveri: Studies in Epigraphy, Archaeology and History*, Chennai, 2001, pp. 331-342.
6. *South Indian Inscriptions* (hereafter *SII*), Publications of the Archaeological Survey of India, vols. I–XXVI, New Delhi, 1890–1990, Vol. III, no. 209, pp. 393-412.
7. *Epigraphia Indica*, (Govt. Pub.) Calcutta/ New Delhi (hereafter EI), 36 vols., 1892-1989, vol. XXXVI, no. 20, p. 153; T. N Subramanian, *Pallavar Seppedugal Muppathu*, Madras, 1967, pp. 186-96.

8. SII, vol. II, 99, pp. 517-21.
9. T.N. Subramanian, *Pallavar Seppedugal Muppathu*, pp. 210-223, lines, 38-222.
10. S. Rajavelu, 'Migration of the Brahmins to Tamilandu under the Pallavas', in S. Rajagopal, ed., *Kaveri: Studies in Epigraphy, Archaeology and History*, pp. 397-407, see pp. 401-403.
11. SII, vol. VII, nos. 801–2; N. Sethuraman had dated the inscription to the year AD 958. For different dates see, K.A. Nilakanta Sastri, *The Colas*, Madras, 1984, pp. 129–135.
12. *Annual Report on Epigraphy* including Indian and South Indian Epigraphy, 1881–1922, 1923–45, 1950–90, New Delhi, (hereafter *ARE*), 208 of 1919.
13. K. G Krishnan, *Karandhai Tamil Sangam Plates of Rajendra Cola I*, Memoirs of Archaeological Society of India, no. 79, Delhi, 1984, verses 65-69, p. 61.
14. *Ibid.*
15. ARE, 5 of 1952-3.
16. *Epigraphia Carnatica*, 26 vols., Bangalore, 1886-1955 (hereafter EC) vol. XII, p. 50.
17. SII, vol. XXVI, 333.
18. R. Tirumalai, 'The Brahmadyeas of Pudukottai District', in R. Tirumalai, *Collected Papers: Studies in South Indian Epigraphy and History (of land organization, development and accounts and select Chola and Pandyan townships)*, Madras, 1994, pp. 162-176.
19. Burton Stein, *Peasant State and Society in Medieval South India*, Delhi, 1980, pp. 150, 308-309, Y. Subbarayalu, *Political Geography of the Chola Country*, Madras, 1973. N. Vedachalam, *Society and Culture of Pandya Nadu Gleaned from Literature and Inscriptions*, Ph.D. Dissertation, Tamil University, 1993.
20. Indira Visvanathan Peterson, 'Sramanas against the Tamilway' in John Cort ed., *Open Boundaries: Jain Communities and Culture in Indian History*, New York, 1998, p. 171; Richer H. Davis, 'The story of Disappearing Jains' in John Cort, ed., ibid., pp. 213-14; Johannes Bronkhorst, *Buddhism in the Shadow of Brahmanism*, Leiden 2011; Giovanni Verardi, *Hardships and Downfall of Buddhism in India*, Delhi, 2011.
21. ARE, 277 of 1913.
22. Noboru Karashima, *South Indian History and Society: Studies from Inscriptions, D 850-1800*, Delhi, 1984, pp. 36-37.
23. SII, vol. V, no. 1409; Nilakanta Sastri, *The Colas*, pp. 578-79.
24. Rajan Gurukkal, 'Non-Brahmana Resistance to the Expansion of Brahmadeyas: The Early Pandya Experience', *Proceedings of the Indian History Congress*, 45th session, Annamalai University, Chidambaram, 1984, pp. 161-63.
25. EI, vol. XVII, no. 16, pp. 298-304; S. Jeyaseela Stephen, *The Land, Peasantry and Peasant Life in India: New Direction and Renewed Debate*, Manak Publications, New Delhi, 2008, pp. 44-45.
26. S. Jeyaseela Stephen, *The Land, Peasantry and Peasant Life in India*, pp. 56-57.
27. EI, vol. XXVI, pp.170-73.

28. T.N. Subramanian, 'Pallankoil Jaina Cooper-Plate Grant of Early Pallava Period', *Transactions of the Archaeological Society of South India*, 1958-59, vol. IV, pp. 41-83, see p. 65.
29. ARE, 216 of 1917.
30. SII, vol. VI, no. 57.
31. SII, vol. VII, no. 416.
32. ARE, 645 of 1916.
33. SII, vol. VI, no. 48.
34. SII, vol. VI, no. 50 and 58.
35. ARE, 1909 (B), no. 315.
36. EI, vol. XXII, no. 33, pp. 205-207.
37. M.D Srinivas, T.G Paramasivam and T. Pushkal, *Thirupporur and Vadakupattu: Eighteenth Century Locality Accounts*, Chennai, 2001, p. 24; David Ludden, *Peasant History in South India*, Delhi, 1993, pp. 24-25; R. Sathyanatha Aiyar, *History of the Nayaks of Madura*, Madras, 1980, pp. 106-108.
38. Hari Rao, ed., *Koil Olugu*, Madras, Rochouse and Sons Pvt. Ltd, 1961, pp. 72-80.
39. SII, vol. II, no.73, pp. 346-51, see verses 23-25, p. 349.
40. K.V. Raman, 'The Sources of Pondicherry's History—Early Period', *Revue Historique de Pondichéry*, vol. XV, 1987, pp. 21–31. It is a copper plate with inscriptions (200 x 90 mm.) discovered at Bahoor in 1879 and now kept in the *Bibliotheque Nationale*, Paris, MSS. Indien, No. 574. See also, C. Minskashi, *Administration and Social Life under the Pallavas*, Madras, 1975, p. 238.
41. ARE, 240 of 1930.
42. ARE, 1918, part II, pp. 146-47.
43. ARE, 176 of 1919.
44. T.A. Gopinatha Rao, ed., *Travancore Archaeological Series*, Madras, 1910-13, vol. I, no. 34, pp. 129-49, see verses, 80-81, pp. 148-9.
45. EI, vol. XIII, p. 142.
46. SII, vol. III, no. 128
47. SII, vol. XIII, p. 243.
48. SII, vol. XIII, p. 243.
49. SII, vol. XXX, p. 142; ARE 97 of 1921.
50. SII, vol. XIII, 110.
51. SII, vol. III, part I, p. 49.
52. SII, vol. III, no. 128
53. SII, vol. VIII, no. 286.
54. S. Subrahmanya Sastry, ed., *Tirumalai-Tirupati Devasthanam Epigraphical Series*, Madras 1931, (hereafter TTDES), vol. I, no. 199-200.
55. SII, vol. XIII, 110.
56. Aa. Sivasubramanian, *Brahaamana Bhojanamum Satti Sorrum: Idaikaala Thamizhagathil Vaithigamum Saathi Uruvakkamum*, 2017, p. 8.
57. ARE, 23 of 1922, 41 of 1911, 227 of 1921, SII, vol. VII, 891, SII, vol. IV, 293.

58. ARE, 218 of 1912.
59. SII, vol. V, 449.
60. ARE, 279 of 1927.
61. A. Krishnan, *Kalvettil Vaazhviyal*, Chennai, 1991, pp. 150-51.
62. ARE, 308 of 1927.
63. SII, vol. IV, 536.
64. ARE, 71 of 1932.
65. SII, vol. V, no. 479.
66. Krishnan, *Kalvettil Vaazhviyal*, pp. 154-55.
67. ARE, 308 of 1927.
68. EI, vol. XXI, no. 21, p. 165.
69. ARE, 577 of 1920.
70. ARE 1909, pp. 82-83.
71. SII, vol. XXVIII, no. 285.
72. ARE, 70 and 71 of 1931-32.
73. ARE, 125 of 1908.
74. IPS, no. 601.
75. ARE, 372 of 1906.
76. Krishnan, *Kalvettil Vaazhviyal*, pp. 138-140; ARE 301, 302, 303 of 1923.
77. ARE, 1909, part II, para 28; ARE, 104 of 1939.
78. Aa. Sivasubramanian, *Brahmahaththi: Varalaarum Vazhakkaarum*, Chennai, 2008, pp. 39-57.
79. P.R. Srinivasan and Marie Louis Reiniche, *Tiruvannamalai, A Saiva Sacred Complex of South India, Inscriptions*, vol.1.1 and 1.2, Pondicherry, 1990, see vol. I, no. 360.
80. ARE, 1909 (B), no. 315.
81. ARE, 297 of 1927.
82. SII, vol. XXIV, no. 192; ARE, 189 of 1927.
83. SII, vol. II, part III, no. 65.
84. K.R. Srinivasa Aiyar, *Inscriptions in the Pudukottai State*, 2 Parts, Pudukottai, 1941-46 (herefater IPS), no. 904.
85. SII, vol. I, no. 56.
86. EI, vol. XVIII, p. 177; ARE 318 of 1919; SII, vol. II, part V, no. 98; SII vol. XII, no. 36; EI vol. VIII, pp. 49-53.
87. S. Jeyaseela Stephen, *Oceanscapes: Tamil Textiles in the Early Modern World*, Delhi, Primus, 2014, pp. 7-9.
88. Ibid.
89. ARE, 308 of 1913; SII, vol. XII, no. 154.
90. Kenneth Hall, *Trade & Statecraft in the Age of the Colas*, New Delhi, 1980, p. 133.
91. ARE, 47 of 1932-33

92. ARE, 538 of 1916-17.

93. Records of Fort St. George, *Diary and Consultation Book*, 1672-1746, 1749-1757, 80 vols., Madras, 1910-53 (hereafter DCB), see 19 November 1694, p. 131.

94. ARE, 286 of 1910; Vijaya Ramasamy, *Textiles and Weavers in Medieval South India*, Delhi, 1985, p. 107; Vijaya Ramasamy, 'Migrations of the Weaver Communities in Medieval Peninsular India: Thirteenth to the Eighteenth Centuries', in Vijaya Ramasamy, ed., *Migrations in Medieval and Early Colonial India*, London, 2016, pp. 165-192.

95. V. Rangachari, *The Inscriptions of the Madras Presidency*, III vols, Madras, 1919, see vol. II, no. 992, pp. 1360-61, see no. 996A (AD 1542); S. Jeyaseela Stephen, *The Coromandel Coast and its Hinterland: Economy, Society and Political System, 1500-1600*, Delhi, 1997, p. 82, pp. 179-180; ARE, 622 of 1915, 201 of 1936-7.

96. Vijaya Ramasamy, 'Traditional Crafts, Technology and Society in Pre-colonial Peninsular India', in Rajat Datta, ed., *Rethinking a Millennium: Perspectives on Indian History from the Eighth to the Eighteenth Century: Essays for Harbans Mukhia*, Delhi, 2008, pp. 275-299; S. Jeyaseela Stephen, Oceanscapes, pp. 558-95.

97. ARE, 291 of 1947-48, 506 of 1958-59, 119 of 1908, 322 of 1927, 70 of 1934-35, 72 of 1934-35, 113 of 1900, 59 of 1933-34, 133 of 1921; SII, vol. VIII, 247, SII, vol. VIII, 750, IPS, no. 454 and 669, ARE, 141 of 1941-42, 201 of 1932-33, 216 of 1930-31, 362 of 1923, 364 of 1911, 276 of 1912, 23 of 1910, 298 of 1910, 17 of 1932-33, 499 of 1926, 35 of 1933-34, 136 of 1924, 89 of 1932-33, 59 of 1933-34, 83 of 1941-42, 137 of 1921, 228 of 1902, 454 of 1921, 623 of 1904.

98. ARE 35 of 1933-34; IPS, no. 486, no. 274, ARE, 1955, p.18, 203 of 1921, 594 of 1893, 248 of 1963-64, 95 of 1924, IPS, no. 325, no. 345, no. 328; SII, vol. XIV, no. 159.

99. Meera Abraham, *Two Medieval Merchant Guilds of South India*, Delhi, 1988, p. 76; EI, vol. VII, pp. 197-198; K. Indrapala, 'South Indian Mercantile Communities in Ceylon, Circa 950-1250', *Journal of Historical and Sociological Studies*, vol. 1, no. 2, July-December 1971, pp. 101-108; Nilakanta Sastri, 'A Tamil Merchant Guild in Sumatra', *Tijdschrift voor Indische Taal-Land und Volkenkunde*, vol. 63, no. 2, 1932, pp. 314-327. Nilakanta Sastri, 'Takuapa and its Tamil Inscription', *Journal of the Malaysian Branch of the Royal Asiatic Society*, vol. 22, no. 1, 1949, pp. 25-30.

100. S. Jeyaseela Stephen, *Portuguese in the Tamil Coast: Historical Explorations in Commerce and Culture, 1507-1749*, Pondicherry, 1998; S. Jeyaseela Stephen, *Expanding Portuguese Empire and the Tamil Economy: Sixteenth-Eighteenth Centuries*, Delhi, 2009.

101. S. Jeyaseela Stephen, *Oceanscapes*, pp. 116-189; Kanakalatha Mukund, *The Trading World of the Tamil Merchant: Evolution of Merchant Capitalism in the Coromandel*, Hyderabad, 1999, see chapter five.

102. S. Jeyaseela Stephen, *Missioner Tamil: Written and Printed in Pondicherry: Literature and Louis Savinien Dupuis, 1841-73*, Pondicherry, 2017, pp. 133-137.

103. Det Kongelige Bibliotheek, Kobenhavn, Mss Call no. Ledr. 389 20: 31 October 1713. Rigsarkivet, Kobenhaven, B. Ziegenbalg and J.E. Grundler, *Mss Diarium und Konferenzbuch, 9 July 1706 -31 December 1719*; Wilhelm Germann, *Ziegenbalg und Plutschau: Die Grundungsjahre der Trankenbarschen Mission: Ein Beitrang zur Geschite des Pietsmus nach handschriftlichen Quellen und altesten Drucken*, 2 vols, Erlangen, 1868, vol. I, p. 236; Arno Lehmann, ed., *Alte Briefe aus Indien: Unveroffentlichte Briefe von Bartholomaus Ziegenbalg, 1706-1719*, Berlin, 1957, p. 310; S. Jeyaseela Stephen, *The First Catholic Bible in Tamil and Louis Savinien Dupuis at Pondicherry: A History of Translation and Printing, 1850-7*, Pondicherry, 2017, pp. 37-38;
104. Paul Olangier, *Les Jesuites a Pondichery et l'affaire Nainiappa, 1705-1720*, Paris, 1932; S. Jeyaseela Stephen, *Pondicherry under the French: Illuminating the Urban Landscape*, Primus, Delhi, 2018.

Chapter - 2

Free Labour and Coolie Migration under the French from Pondicherry and Karaikal to Mauritius and Reunion and the Social Life of the Tamils in the Colonies, 1729-1883

Artisans were brought from Pondicherry to Mauritius in the ship La Sirene on 4 March 1729. They have signed deeds of contract as early as in 1734. On 9 April 1734 Appan Canaury the artisan from Pondicherry had signed a contract to work in Mauritius. There are also other similar artisans who had signed contracts like Raman and Vellai Savariappan. These skilled workers of Tamil origin migrated were also employed to train the African slave work force. Labourers who were skilled were recruited on contract system for a period of three years by the French in Pondicherry were transported from Cuddalore to Pondicherry and brought in ships continuously owing to demand in the French colonies of Mauritius, Le Reunion and the Comoros. The French East India Company had resorted to this well developed process of skilled labour recruitment through contracts as early as in 1775. Many Tamil carpenters migrated and they were employed at Port Louis in Mauritius. Master craftsmen who were mostly Tamil Hindus also migrated from Cuddalore. It became an established practice that masons, carpenters, dock-workers and sailors were employed on a contract for three years in Mauritius. Since 1776, we find also many complaints that were lodged by many Tamil migrant families (like Thaandavarayan, Arunachalam and Chinna Raman). In 1776 a number of complaints had been lodged from those who signed contracts hailing Pondicherry and the various families included were mentioned such as Arunachalam, Pakkiry and Chinna Raman.

Those Tamils who signed contracts were engaged mainly in doing jobs including building works. In spite of such violation of labour contract system and problems faced, we find surprisingly as many as sixteen agreements of labour contracts signed in 1783 between Laurent La Coste and various groups of skilled workers and artisans in Pondicherry who had come in ships to Mauritius. Offering free passage, monetary wages and food rations in Mauritius had been neatly mentioned in these agreements. Terms and conditions were not strictly adhered to as a result some enlightened workers like Rudra Chetti and Sagaadevan headed a legal battle and they severely campaigned for redressal of their grievances.[1]

Three French vessels sailed from Pondicherry to the Mascarenes Islands with 1,200 skilled labourers in 1792.[2] The French Company was able to obtain plenty of artisans from the area of Cuddalore, and, therefore, 2 more French ships sailed away from Pondicherry with 300 Tamils, and they arrived in Mauritius on 3 February 1792.[3] Thus a high degree of labour recruitment and mobility is visible and we find masons, carpenters and blacksmiths had signed the contracts with signatures in Tamil.

The letter of Sir Charles Oakley, the English Governor at Madras in 1792 is interesting to note. He diplomatically refrained from accusing the Dutch for exporting plenty of slaves in the past. He succinctly pointed out that the new system introduced by the Dutch wherein they had given permits to natives who were appointed as contractors to recruit the skilled labourers required. As a result, these labour contractors were active to locate and find out the skilled labourers for export.[4] This is significantly a new development where skilled labour recruitment came up with fixed rules and specific period. Thus locals began to emerge to satisfy the constant demand of the labour needs of the Europeans around the globe and across the seas. Thus by the end of the eighteenth century when slave migrations were stopped and slave trade was abolished, the labour contract system and migration of Tamils to overseas took a new turn.

It is known to us that *sepoys* (soldiers) of Tamil origin were employed in Mauritius and we find Pierre Anna Pragasam was the sergeant of the *sepoys* in 1791.[5] Tamils were largely employed in the construction of Port Louis and its ship yards. In 1785 several Tamils testified before the police in Port Louis calling for the release of Aadiya Paatham the Tamil who was kidnapped by Jean de Silva.[6] A sizeable group of the Tamil migrants had owned a plots of land in the 'Camp de Malabars' (Tamil quarters) and a few had received large grants of land in the rural areas. We come to know nothing of the caste system that existed there at that time.

Over a period of time Tamils who migrated from Pondicherry had become important figures. They were traders, money lenders and property developers in Mauritius. In 1791 we find Jean-Baptiste Arulanandan was said to be employed as the main interpreter. The record of 27 June 1806 mentions that Muthusamy Mudaliar and Thiruselva Pillai were employed as brokers. Savari Muthu Arulanandan was said to be a merchant as per a record of 7 October 1806. Amuthan Joseph and Venkatachalam were teachers of Tamil children in the school.[7] Many of the Tamils had become wealthy. Gnaanapragasam had sold one acre of land in exchange for a plot of land at Pamplmousses Street in Port Louis to Subramanian a Tamil mason and his wife as per the record of 16th day of the republican month Brumaire of the 13th year (1799). Muthu Kumaran the mason in the department of public works had given the right of authorization to Abraham Arulanandan so as to sell his house as per the record of 23rd of the republican month of Prairal of the 10th year (1796). Further, Chidambaram had been described in the record as a mason working in the workshop of the department of works while Karuppan is described as a Tamil goldsmith. Francis Thamby occupied the important rank of sergeant in the army.

Camp de Malabar that emerged in the suburb of Port Louis in Mauritius became important area where the Tamils lived with families. An official recognition was given to the area through an order of 25 October 1803 issued by the General. The settlement had the population mostly of the masons, carpenters, plumbers, cabinet-makers and sailors. The term lascar was used for a sailor and these people were mostly Muslims. Khader was appointed the chief of the lascars in 1780.[8]

In the Camp de Malabar, the people had their own slaves and about 75 per cent of the Tamils generally owned three slaves while a few others had even six slaves by the census of 1804. There were 371 Tamils identified in this census of 1804 based on their names and other available information.[9] Among the slaves there were 316 manumitted adult slaves during 1796-1800 and a break-up of the 46 Indians shows that there were 28 Tamils (besides 9 Telugus and 35 Bengalis).[10]

Religious and Social Practices of Tamil Hindus, Christians and Muslims in Mauritius

Hindu Tamil migrants like Pichai, Latchumanan, Thaandavamorthy and Thaanappa who had become Christians in 1739 and they were baptized and later got married in the churches. Muslim lascars had asserted before the notary in 1806 that Zakir and Abdullah had not been registered in the civil register of Mauritius because they were bachelors and had remained unmarried and so could not get registered their names in the registers.[11] Tamil Christians attended the church services in French and it was the parish Church of St. Louis. The wish of the Tamils to have an independent church with divine services for worship came to be fulfilled only in 1823 when the administration accorded sanction for building a chapel. The Tamil Muslims had a mosque built in 1806 when the administration granted a piece of land. Hindus did not have a temple for long and the first temple at Terre Rouge in Mauritius was built in 1816. Another temple was built when the Tamil merchants purchased a plot of land on 25 October 1856. A group of Tamil merchants had appeared before Mr Macquet the notary of grand Port–Savanne for registration of the plot of land for building the Hindu temple.[12]

The customs and manners of the Tamils in Mauritius had been depicted in records. It was a great offence to touch the moustache while cutting the hair of a Hindu slave.[13] Women wore sarees, blouse and skirts and were bedecked with jewellery like ear-ring, nose-stud, pendants, ring for the hand and foot-fingers, bracelets for the arms and legs, and thaali the wedding cord.[14] The decoration of the hair by women with fresh flowers was a daily practice. The Tamils used at home *thambalam* (brass plates) *sombu* (copper pots) and earthern utensils. They also used a spitting bowl because they chewed the betel leaves.[15]

It was a social practice found among Tamils in Mauritius that the funeral processions were attended by a wide concourse of friends. Hindu rites were observed by the Hindus. Flowers were thrown on the coffin. Prayers in Tamil were recited in the graveyard before burial. The Muslims read a few verses form Koran.[16] The Catholics took the dead to bury in the Christian cemetery.[17]

Music and dance was popular among the Tamils and they were allowed to sing and dance before eleven o' clock in the night. These dances were very noisy.[18] One of the dances was *kollaattum* to gather in circle and they used pieces of wood. D'Unienville the French official found that Tamil slaves sang lugubrious songs and their dance looked more like a pantomime.[19] Presence of Tamil jugglers had also been noted in Mauritius by Milbert another traveller.

The free Tamils and the ex-slave Tamils contacted endogamous marriages and there emerged many Tamil families who were related to one another. Such families like Venkata Subramanian, Muththaya and Perumal are noted in French records.[20] Account books and promissory notes were written in Tamil. Savari Muthu the father of a Tamil family had signed in Tamil in a record while his son who was educated in French had signed in the document in French. Thus education of the next generation is important to note.[21]

Jacques Denis Pichchai was appointed the head of the Tamils in Mauritius. He was paid an annual salary of 1200 *livres*. He was commended for his intelligence and probity.[22] There was another person Ignaasi to assist him and his salary was fixed at 840 livres per annum.[23] There was a Tamil chief peon who was held responsible for selecting and recruiting people for employment in the administration.[24] It is important to note that the Tamils had *naadu* (an assembly) of their own with the elders of their community. It had also its own rules and regulations.[25] The members of the *naadu* called *naattar* heard cases of disputes and settled them amicably and also imposed fines and punishments. The assembly was denounced by the French police for acting as a law court. At one of its evening session, the 24 members present were all arrested.[26] The *naattars* were no longer allowed to hold such assembly. The colonial government imposed its own form of organization the Syndicate of the Tamils. The post of chief peon was upgraded to the chief of the Syndicate of Tamils under the French administration and the chief peon was added with new responsibilities to govern the Tamils.[27] Thus new colonial policy came to be introduced and followed. Michael Savari Muthu was appointed in 1823 as the official interpreter of Tamil language by the administration in Mauritius. Education to Tamils was provided by opening a colonial academy in Mauritius.

The Tamil population over a period time declined in Mauritius because most of them returned after the expiry of the terms of labour contract of five years. Some had renewed and stayed. There were Tamils who wished to settle down in Mauritius and wished not to return to Pondicherry for they had acquired properties. We find that 188 households with 270 children by 1804. There were only 36 married couples with an average of four children in 1804.[28] Many Tamil families had returned to Pondicherry with their children while in some cases the head of the family alone stayed and worked in Mauritius. Charles Kulandai was one who sent back his wife and children to Pondicherry. Ramaputhiran also did the same and when he died in Mauritius his children were in Pondicherry. Abraham Arulanandan a trustworthy Tamil had been given several proxies to proceed with the sale of property of those who had left Mauritius. However, those who left Mauritius and again wanted to settle in the Island later and carry on trade were never accorded permission by the French East India Company. By 1812, Reunion (Bourbon) and Mauritius were in British hands and the Napoleonic Empire was collapsing.

It must be also pointed out that the slave trade from South India, though on a relatively small scale also formed part of colonial plantation economy in Mauritius at the end of the eighteenth century. The Dutch had begun the direct slave trade from South India to Mauritius. In the late eighteenth century, slaves from South India were regularly sold to French planters in Mauritius and Reunion. A proclamation by the British Governor-General was made in 1789 prohibiting the export of slaves. There were some 6,000 Indian slaves in Mauritius and 2,000 in Reunion by 1800.[29]

The Immigration of Coolies from Pondicherry and Karaikal to Reunion Island under the French, 1841-1883

The French in Reunion desired to have coolie labourers from Pondicherry for the sugar plantations. Their concern stemmed, at least in part, from the late 1820s. It witnessed their attempts to recruit free Tamil agricultural laborers to work on Reunion.[30] Arrangements were therefore made and ships sailed from Pondicherry and Karaikal transporting coolies. Tamils and others from various parts of India who reached were about 3,000 by 1830. The legal rules in force provided that the coolies should receive food, lodging and wages. In practice, however, the employer-landowners seldom complied with the rules and in the event of a dispute or a problem with the administration, the settlers justified withholding the wages of the Indian coolies by claiming that they had failed to fulfill their commitments. The arguments invoked were quite similar to those used with regard to the labour of domestic servants in France in the nineteenth century.

The cultivated land area in cane sugar producing colony of Reunion in 1826 was 8,241 hectares. It had increased in 1836 to 14,530 hectares and in 1839 it was 22,405.[31] Owing to demand in labour the French encouraged coolies from Pondicherry and Karaikal. The English in Madras noted the large scale migrants and also reported the details. It is found mention in 1841 that Sivanadiyaan in Karaikal was tracked by his wife down to the warehouse where he was lodged and confined. She learnt that the husband waited for the ship from Pondicherry to be transported as an indentured labourer. She showed her contempt for what she considered his poor choice by dramatically throwing on the ground the precious rupees which he had secured as an advance. The money for the release was passed through a crack in the door and finally she managed to get her husband.[32] Thus it is gleaned that labour recruitment by the French was extensively carried out through the agents.

A new decree was adopted in 1843 in Reunion to regulate the migration of coolies. Their contracts were supposed to last at least five years and the minimum age of the coolie was set at 16. The landowners had to agree to pay wages and also for the return trip. Ill treatment or a two-month delay in wage payments was sufficient grounds for the administration to nullify a contract.[33] By tightening the legal rules in favour of the coolies, the French administration hoped to solve the problem of labour shortage and those social issues raised by the Tamil coolies. However, once again, estate owners seemed unwilling to comply with the rules.[34] Those coolies recruited were transported in the ships that sailed from Pondicherry and Karaikal in 1844 and in 1845.[35] It is known that 581 emigrants sailed in a ship that left Karaikal and reached Reunion Island in 1848. In the next year many ships sailed and brought 4161 coolies and in 1850 ships continued to sail and brought 2183 coolies to Reunion.[36]

In 1849 the contract was signed between François Allen the captain of the ship Graham and Louis Chasteau of Port Louis in Mauritius who was acting for Vinay & Company of Pondicherry for the supply of coolies. As per the terms Francois Allen was to go and visit three ports of the Coromandel Coast and address his travel to Vinay & Company and their agents, at each of the three ports and embark in the ship with a maximum of 230 labourers, for which he was to receive 800 dollars towards the cost of the shipment.[37] The Madras Spectator on 19 September 1849 reported and it blamed the French in Pondicherry for its competition in recruiting coolies for Reunion Islands and it stated the drop in numbers going to Mauritus under the British which fell from an average of 853 per month to 550 per month.[38] Governor Pujol, requested legal protections to be followed strictly in favour of the immigrants.[39] Other colonial administrators and plantation owners thought this state of affairs was due to Indian indolence rather than to contracts of engagement and lack of cooperation among landowners.

Coolie Immigrants from Karaikal to Reunion, 1851-62

Year	*Number of Migrants*
1851	1988
1852	1833
1853	1472
1854	3206

(Contd...)

1855	757
1856	258
1857	934
1858	312
1859	1128
1860	448
1861	768
1862	1370
Total	**14474**

Source: Roucaia Badat, *Un Comptoir francais des Indes: Karaikal de 1850 a 1862*, Memoire de maitrise d'histoire, Universite de Aix-en-Provence, 1972,pp. 111-2.

The French in Pondicherry made efforts to recruit coolie labourers from the suburbs of the town and in the hinterland. They were successful in transporting 8078 coolies in ships in 1849 and 6598 coolies in ships in the year 1850 to Reunion Island. The Society of Emigration in Pondicherry was set up in 1851 and it facilitated easily the recruitment and export of coolies. Louis Le Faucheur, Arunachalam and Sabapathi had mainly recruited coolies for Reunion Island. On 4 January 1851 they accepted the society's new contract given to them for recruitment of coolies. They also concluded a new agreement and signed a contract on 10 February 1853. According to the practice, the Society of Emigration met the expenditure towards the preparation of the contract deed, making the passport for the individual, cost of medical checkup, his livelihood, maintenance or superintendence in the warehouse or place of stay and embarkation till boarding the ship. The rates were fixed for transporting coolies for the Reunion. As on 25 April 1855 the price fixed was 39 rupees towards a single individual. Other than Society of Emigration, the labour recruitment was also done and if work was undertaken by the authorized concerned agents the amount fixed for sending a coolie to Reunion islands was 41 rupees. Thus there was a difference of 2 rupees which had to be borne by the agent. The condition of coolies who arrived in Reunion was said to be satisfactory to humanity by Dr. Monatt and his opinion was quoted in 'Friend of India' journal on 23 September 1852. The market for coolie was far from being 'free', not only because of diplomatic and political interference but also because of the way it worked. In the early 1850s, the rules adopted in France were increasingly favourable to workers (e.g. the law prohibiting child labour, the abolition of a criminal charge for forming workers' coalitions). The Second Empire imposed tighter restrictions on emancipated slaves and coolies. A contract of labour was a must and it was imposed in 1852 on all workers in the colonies. The legal rules governing were widely implemented and enforced.[40] Anyone without fixed employment defined as a job lasting more than one year was considered a vagrant and punished as such in 1852.[41] The penalties were considerable, but the law was also frequently circumvented through fictitious contracts of engagements that some–especially women–signed with landowners who were interested in having occasional labourers.[42]

The French had by that time shipped around 20,000 labourers who had reached Reunion.[43] The Society of Emigration in Pondicherry recruited Tamil labourers and we find details in French records from 1851 to 1860 who reached Reunion.

Coolie Immigrants from Pondicherry to Reunion, 1851-60

Year	*Migrants*
1851	4107
1852	3383
1853	3181
1854	9135
1855	3097
1856	2233
1857	1449
1858	1324
1859	2394
1860	1150
Total	31453

Source: Lucien Wickers, *L'immigration reglementee a Ile de la Reunion*, Doctoral thesis, Paris, 1911, p. 46.

The statistics provided above shows that the coolie labour recruitment and transport in ships from Pondicherry to Reunion was higher than that of Karaikal which was almost triple in nature. In some French documents the number of emigrants actually boarded in ships from Pondicherry to Reunion had been given. We find mention of 122 emigrants in 1857 and 203 in 1858 except Karaikal. Ubraye, the French Governor of Pondicherry limited the recruitment of coolies in the months of April, May June 1859. Thereafter the recruitment began again for Reunion islands in July 1859.[44]

Some records also throw light on the emigration of coolies by gender and classification. It is found in 1858 that 463 men, 32 women, infants between the age of five and twelve were 11 and the children above 12 years of age were 9 who all had sailed in a ship to Reunion Island. Thus the ship carried 515 emigrants in total.[45]

Labour recruitment of coolies had been very active in Pondicherry in 1859 and as a result large scale migration took place to Reunion. Eight ships had carried 2,394 coolie emigrants. It is also interesting to note that there were coolies recruited in Karaikal and Pondicherry but owing to some reasons they dropped themselves from boarding the ships. The number of coolies was 349, 141, 147, 139, 450 and 88 respectively in the years 1854, 1855, 1856, 1857, 1858 and 1859. Thus the total fallout had been 1314 coolies in six years.[46]

Labour Migration in 1859 from Pondicherry to Reunion

Date of departure	*Name of the ship*	*Number of persons*
25 February 1859	George	200
20 April 1859	Foi	240
9 May 1859	Marie-Laure	300
24 May 1859	Laurence	290
June 1859	Elizabeth	447
August 1859	Foi	257
Before November	-	186
Before December	Pamplemousses	474
Total		**2, 394**

Source: Letter du Gouverneur d'Ubraye au Minister du 26 Juillet 1859, no. 328; Etat recapitulatif des emigrants de tous age, embarque de Pondichery et de Karikal sur les navires de la compagnie generale maritime du 1er Janvier au 28 Octobre 1859.

The arrival of coolies by the ship Pamplemousses in 1859 was said to be 438 and so 36 persons died on voyage. Further the arrival of coolies by the ship Foi was 255 and so 2 persons had died on voyage. Labour recruitment continued in 1860 and 3 ships sailed with 1150 coolies to Reunion.

Coolie Immigrants from Pondicherry to Reunion, 1860

Date/year	*Ship name*	*Persons*
19 April 1860	Junon	361
12 June 1860	Maupertius	369
2 July 1860	Santiago	420
Total		**1150**

Source: ANSOM, Inde 466, Dossier 600, Etat recapitulatif des engages embarques des repenses, des recettes et des benefices faits par la Societe d'Emigration suivant ses livres du 27 Juin 1859 au 23 Mai 1861; ANSOM, Inde 466, Dossier 600, Letter of Ubraye of 10 October 1860, no. 147 and 2 November 1860 of no. 502, Note sur la emigration a la Reunion en 1860, *Revue Coloniale*, 1861, p. 362.

Return of the Coolies from Reunion to French India, 1849-60

It is interesting to find in records that the coolies on expiry of the terms of contract returned regularly in ships to French India. But the exclusive mention of return to Pondicherry and Karaikal had not been neatly found mention. The statistics neatly shows that one fourth of the coolies had only returned after the expiry of contracts while one thirds of labourers stayed and lived in Reunion Island.

Return of Coolies from Reunion to Pondicherry and Karaikal, 1849-60

Year	*Coolies*
1849	160
1850	163
1851	130
1852	135
1853	475
1854	1410
1855	2009
1856	1120
1857	1114
1858	918
1859	1148
1860	875
Total	**9657**

Source: ANSOM, Carton de la Reunion 454, Dossier 5074, Etat des immigrants nes. repatries et morts a la Reunion depuis 1848 et jusqu' en 1866, fait a Paris le 21 Mai 1867 pour les annee posterieures a 1866, ont et e utilisees les statistiques des dossiers Reunion, 5058 (Annee 1867) a 5073 (Annee 1883).

Labour Immigration to Reunion since 1861

In 1861 the ship Jeune Albert sailed with 437 coolies to Reunion. Another ship carried 382 coolies in the same year. Hence a total of 819 had emigrated. The emigrants from Pondicherry to Reunion had continued from 1861 to 1882 and we have the statistics. It is found that no shipment of coolies was carried out during the years 1867, 1868, 1870, 1871, 1872, 1876 and 1877.

Immigration of Coolies from Pondicherry to Reunion islands, 1861-82

Year	*Migrants*
1861	819
1862	1595
1863	295
1864	830
1865	461
1866	986
1869	784
1873	611
1874	643
1875	363
1878	145
1879	837
1880	895
1881	244
1882	813
Total	**10321**

Source: ANSOM, Reunion 454, Tableau construit avec les statistiques dos dossiers, 5052 (Annee 1861) et 5072 (Annee 1882)

Ships began to sail from Madras to Reunion carrying coolies during 1863 and 1865. This had been noted in the French records.

Immigration of Coolies from Madras to Reunion islands 1863-1865

Year	*Migrants*
1863	797
1864	1553
1865	224
Total	**2574**

Source: ANSOM, Reunion 454, Tableau construit avec les statistiques dos dossiers, 5054 (Annee 1863) et 5056 (Annee 1865)

Labour recruitment in Karaikal continued and the ships began to sail from Karaikal to Reunion carrying coolies during 1861 and 1882. However, no shipping of coolies was carried out during the year 1867, 1868, 1870, 1871, 1872, 1876 and 1877.

Immigration of Coolies from Karaikal to Reunion islands 1861-1882

Year	*Migrants*
1861	489
1862	1044
1863	349
1864	348
1865	242
1866	495
1869	297
1873	425
1874	501
1875	326
1888	158
1879	736
1880	795
1881	381
1882	461
Total	**7047**

Source: ANSOM, Reunion 454, Tableau construit avec les statistiques des dossiers, 5052 (Annee 1861) et 5072 (Annee 1882)

Labour recruitment agencies were active in Pondicherry and Karaikal and so it facilitated the transport to Reunion between 1861 and 1869. However it gleaned that no ships sailed carrying coolies in 1867, 1868, 1870, 1871 and 1872.

Labour Migration through Agencies in Pondicherry and Karaikal to Reunion, 1861-69

Year	*Migrants*
1861	1384
1862	2639
1863	644
1864	1178
1865	703
1866	1481
1869	1081
Total	**9110**

Source: ANSOM, Reunion 454, Tableau construit avec les statistiques des dossiers, 5052 (Annee 1861), 5057 (Annee 1866) and 5060 (Annee 1869)

Coolies continued to recruited and so ships sailed carrying coolies to Reunion between 1873 and 1882. However, it is gleaned that no ships sailed carrying coolies in 1876 and 1877. Some Tamil women from Mauritius sought to escape from abusive or unhappy conjugal relationships to Reunion Island in 1880. We find a case wherein Lakshmi Shengaalin (Lachoomii Chengelayen) ran away from Mauritius to the neighbouring island of Reunion, with Ramasamy Ramalingam to escape from her estranged husband, Venkatachalam Appu. He nevertheless subsequently sought his wife's extradition, noting that she had not only abandoned her three-year old child but had taken a wooden box containing one hundred rupees and ten sovereigns of five dollars each, four gold earrings and one gold ring.[47] The migration of coolies from Pondicherry to Reunion was finally suspended by the French Governor in 1883.

Immigration of Coolies from Pondicherry and Karaikal to Reunion, 1873-1882

Year	*Migrants*
1873	1036
1874	1144
1875	689
1878	303
1879	1573
1880	1690
1881	625
1882	1274
Total	**8334**

Source: ANSOM, Reunion 454, Tableau construit avec les statistiques des dossiers, 5064 (Annee 1873) et 5072 (Annee 1882)

Return of the Coolies from Reunion to French India, 1861-83

On expiry of the terms of contract the coolie labourers returned in ships from Reunion to Pondicherry and Karaikal from 1861 to 1883 except in the year 1870.

Return of the Coolies from Reunion to Pondicherry and Karaikal, 1861-83

Year	*Coolies*
1861	639
1862	858
1863	759

(Contd...)

1864	618
1865	246
1866	1357
1867	799
1868	450
1869	502
1871	305
1872	178
1873	597
1874	389
1875	367
1876	151
1877	32
1878	1639
1879	1739
1880	1531
1881	1321
1882	772
1883	169
Total	**15418**

Source: ANSOM, Carton de la Reunion 454, Dossier 5074, Etat des immigrants nes Repatries et morts a la Reunion depuis 1848 et jusqu' en 1866, fait a Paris le 21 Mai 1867 pour les annee posterieures a 1866, ont et e utilisees les statistiques des dossiers Reunion, 5058 (Annee 1867) a 5073 (Annee 1883)

To conclude it may be said that the labour system developed under the French in the beginning in Pondicherry was that a sailor was rewarded for enlisting artisans overseas. But later developments led to a contract signing when migrant workers on a large scale were recruited which became thus a common contractual form in the labour market for plantation economy. It may be mentioned that 87,083 coolie labourers had signed contracts and emigrated from Pondicherry and Karaikal to work in the plantations in Reunion Island from 1849 to 1882. However, we find 25,075 coolie labourers in total had returned on expiry of the contracts from Reunion to Pondicherry during 1849 and 1883. It shows that more than two thirds had preferred to stay back or compelled to remain owing to some reasons and did not or could not return to Tamil country their motherland. In the records what we find the main reason was that they could not pay off the debts incurred with the contractors. Hence they were again indentured themselves for a further extension period of contract.

The French had derived the notion and practice of 'wage earner' called coolie just derived from Tamil language. But over a period of time and experimentation with the system it became a peculiar form, the indentured labour. The contract was derivative of two already existing systems that of the sailor and that of the artisans besides another that of the contacts between the agrarian labourer/wage earner and the French East India Company. The planters in the colonies had ill treated the workers in the plantations by extracting labour for working long hours than the specified hours as recorded in the contract deed. The place of stay was not comfortable at all. They were given minimum food and clothing and there was no proper medical aid. The coolies were sold and resold in the plantations for 2000 francs to 3000 francs. It may be mentioned that the subaltern studies have generally argued that colonial legal constructions were a tool for dominating peripheries of the empires. At the outset it should be outlined that the imperial tensions linked to the circulation of notions and practices of labour were complex and also had uncertain consequences. The coolie system emerged in the beginning under the French was a mixture of various labour systems and stood somewhere between slavery and free wage labour.

Notes

1. Marina Carter, *Veils from Indenture: Experiences of Indian Migrants in the British Empire*, Leicester University Press, London, 1996, p. 90.
2. British Library (hereafter BL), London, Oriental and India office Collection (hereafter OIOC), P/241/31, fol. 562, see the letter of Mathew Yeats to Sir Charles Oakley dated 22 December 1792.
3. BL, OIOC, P/241/36, fols.16–19, see the letter of Mathew Yeats to Major-General William Meadows dated 3 February 1792.
4. BL, OIOC, P/252/76, fl.791, see the letter of Charles Oakley to Jacob Eilbracht dated 14 February 1792
5. National Archives of Mauritius (hereafter NAM), Journal de Police, Série JL, 18-27 Juin 1791.
6. NAM, 058, Série Z, Bureau de Police (Jurisdiction Royale), Journal pour la consignation des rapports de police 15 Avril 1785-31 Mars 1787, fl.285.
7. NAM, Série E, 17b, Comite de surete publique 1793-1803.
8. NAM, Série Z, 2B, no. 20, Jurisdiction Royale, Register des audiences de police tenues par le Juge Royal, 22 Decembre 1773-25 Mars, 1780.
9. NAM, Série K, KK3, Census of 1804.
10. NAM, Série A, A41, Register pour server a l'enregisterement des actes d'affranchissement accordes aux esclaves de Port-Louis, Municipalite de Port-Louis, 1796-1800, fl. 253.
11. NAM, Minutes de notaire, J.F. Arnaud, Série N, NA 38/12 c , 22 fevrier 1806-11-Avril 1807.

12. Land deen Notary Macquet, 25 Octobre 1856, Reg. C88, No.1650, March 1863, register Série A, A.143, no.276.
13. J.G. Milbert, *Voyage Pictoresque a L'Ile de France, au Cap de Bonne Esperance et a L'Ile de Teneriffe*, II vols., Paris, 1812, p. 187.
14. J.G. Milbert, Voyage Pictoresque, p. 173; NAM, Minutes de notaire L.D. Durand, Inventaire après le deces de Maria Saron, veuve Chavriage An 9, Série N, vol. NA 50/10 B.
15. NAM, Minutes de notaire L.D. Durand, Inventaire après le deces de Maria saron, veuve Chavriage An 9 Série N, vol. NA 50/10 B.
16. J. G. Milbert, *Voyage Pictoresque*, p. 186.
17. NAM, Série O, OA 85, Bureau de Police (Instruction Royale), Livre pour server a L'enregisterment de divers orders, letters et autres pieces ayant trait aux functions de police, 22 Novembre 1799- 14 Avril 1787, fl. 88.
18. J. G. Milbert, *Voyage Pictoresque*, p. 181.
19. Baron d' Unienville, *Statistique de L'Ile Maurice et ses Dependences*, Paris, tome I, 1838.
20. NAM, Série J, JL 24, Conseilde famille, 7 Floreal An Onze.
21. NAM, Série E, E17B, Comite de surete publique, Register des cautionnements 1797-1803.
22. NAM, Série O, OA 85, Bureau de Police, Jurisdiction Royale, 12 Avril 1785.
23. NAM, Série G, GA2, Gouvernment Imperial, p. 9
24. NAM, Série O, OA 85, 9 Decembre 1786.
25. NAM, Série Z, 2B/20, Audience de la Police 22 Decembre 1793-25 Mars 1780.
26. NAM, Série Z, 2B/20, Audience de la Police, 22 Decembre 1773-25, Mars 1780.
27. NAM, Série O, OA/85, 7 Juin 1784.
28. NAM, Série K, KK3, Census of 1804.
29. D.R. Banerji, *Slavery in British India*, Second edition, 1933, pp. 59, 171. Hubert Gerbeau, 'Engagees and Coolies on Reunion Island: Slavery's Masks and Freedom's Constraints', in P.C. Emmer ed., *Colonialism and Migration: Indentured Labour before and after Slavery*, Dordrecht, 1986, p. 211; Hugh Tinker, *A New System of Slavery: The Export of Indian Labour Overseas, 1830-1920*, 1974, p. 44.
30. Jacques Weber, 'L'emigration indienne a` La Reunion: 'Contraire a` la morale' ou 'utile a` l'humanite'? (1829–1860)', in *Esclavage et abolitions dans l'ocean Indien, 1723–1860*, ed., Edmond Maestri, Paris, L'Harmattan, 2002, pp. 309–10; see also, Jacques Weber, *Les Etablissements français en Inde au XIXe Siècle (1816-1914),* Paris, 5 vols, Paris, 1988.
31. Louis-Napoléon Bonaporte, *Analyse de la Question des Sucres*, Administration de Librairie, Paris, 1842, p. 10.
32. BL, British Parliamentary Papers (hereafter BPP), 1841 (45), Calcutta Commission of Enquiry Report, Exhibit no. 21, p. 138; BL, Oriental and India Office Collection (hereafter OIOC), *Madras Public Proceedings* (hereafter MPP), Statement of Saivaroodian, Madras Police Office, 1842.

33. Bulletin Officiel de l'Ile Bourbon, Arrete du 10 Novembre 1843, p. 354.
34. Centre des Archives de Outre-Mer (hereafter CAOM), Aix-en-Provence, Série F, FM SG/Reu c 406, c 432 d 4603 a' 4606
35. M.G. A de Challaye, 'Memoire sur L'immigration des Indiens et sur le travail libre dans le colonies de Maurice et de Bourbon', *Revue Coloniale*, Tome III, 1ere Série, May-August 1844, pp. 557-609; See also, Immigration des coolies aux reunion, *Revue Coloniale*, 6 Decembre 1845, p. 436; Emigration des coolies aux Mascareignes, *Revue Coloniale*, Mars 1845, pp. 276-98
36. Immigration des coolies aux reunion, *Revue Coloniale*, Septembre-Decembre 1849, p. 320.
37. Archives Nationales, Section Outre-Mer (hereafter ANSOM), Paris, Serie Geographique, Inde, 464/590, see the letter of the Governor of Pondicherry to the Ministere de la Marine dated 1 December 1849.
38. Jacques Weber, *Les Etablissements français en Inde au XIXe Siècle (1816-1914),* Paris, 5 vols, Paris, 1988, see vol. IV, p. 1052.
39. CAOM, Série F, FM SG Inde 464, d. 590, lettre 26 February 1848.
40. Le Moniteur de la Reunion, 3 July 1852.
41. Bulletin Officiel de l'ýle de la Reunion, 13 February 1852.
42. Archives Departementales de la Reunion (hereafter ADR), Saint-Denis, U 339, 349
43. V. Lalitha, 'Emigration of British Subjects from French Ports in India to French Colonies-Proposal to Legalise – Papers Relating to Down to 1858', *Revue Historique de Pondichery*, no. XIII, 1976 - 80, pp. 162-168, pp. 162-3.
44. ANSOM, Inde 466, Dossier 600, Letter no. 380, of August 1859 by d'Ubraye to Ministre.
45. ANSOM, Inde 466, Dossier, 600, P.V. de la séance du 16 Octobre 1858 du conseil administration.
46. Anne-Marie Brahy, *L'Etude des Coolies trade pour les Mascareignes de 1830 a 1865*, Memoire de maitrise, Aix-en-Provence, 1972, p. 83.
47. NAM, PA Series: Letters received by the Protector of Immigrants from other Government Departments, PA 43, Petition of Vencatachellum Appoo dated 23 August 1880; see also, Immigration Department Report dated 1 September 1880.

Chapter - 3

Indenture Labour Tamil Migrants from Pondicherry and Karaikal to the French West Indies and the Life Style in the Sugar Plantations, 1851-90

The French had opened ports in Martinique and Guadeloupe in 1763 to foreign vessels and in Saint-Lucia and the Saint-Domingue (modern day Haiti) in 1767. The free ports acted as collection centres of foreign cotton cultivated in the West Indies. Dominican Islands attracted trade from Martinique and Guadeloupe.[1] The arrangement proved lucrative for British cotton importers. According to one estimate, British subjects could procure French-grown cotton 30 per cent cheaper through West Indian free ports than directly from France.[2] In 1793-95 troops overtook the French islands of Tobago, Martinique, and Trinidad, and briefly held St. Lucia and Guadeloupe. French forces never caused as big a threat to British West Indian colonies and Caribbean shipping in the 1790s. France under the Jacobins as First Republic abolished slave trade in the throes of revolution on 4 February 1794. Pressured by private French slave trading companies, Napoleon Bonaparte reinstated the trade in 1804. At negotiations for the Treaty of Paris (1814), Charles Maurice de Talleyrand in principle agreed to abolition, securing a five-year grace period during which the French held a monopoly on the slave trade to the French colonies. Without public statement in August 1815 Louis XVIII advised all French ports not to authorize outgoing voyages of slave ships and issued decrees to the same effect in following years. Nevertheless, clandestine traffic in slaves continued. Slave trading was stopped in Bordeaux city in France in 1826, but only after an estimated 500 expeditions from there. In 1817 and 1818, laws prohibited the arrival of slave ships in the French West Indies, but did not prevent sales of slaves already there.[3]

African slaves who had been brought to the French Caribbean alone totaled at least 1.6 million, with slave populations peaking in Saint-Domingue at 480,000 in 1791, in Martinique at 86,300 in 1831, in French Guiana at 19,100 in 1831, and in Guadeloupe at 99,500 in 1832.[4] Revolts of slaves occurred in Guadeloupe and Martinique in the early decades of the nineteenth century, including serious disturbances in 1822, 1824, 1831, and 1833.[5] The French had paid great attention to cultivation of cane sugar in the Caribbean Islands and the cultivated land area in Martinique in 1826 was 17,621hectares. It had increased to 23,777 hectares in 1836 and after three years in 1839 in had decreased to 19,814 hectares. Similarly in Guadeloupe it was 22,909 hectares in 1826 and 24,573 hectares in 1836 and it was 20,984 hectares in 1839. Further in French Guiana it was 797 hectares in 1826 and 1,571 hectares in 1836 and 1,305 hectares in 1839.[6]

Slaves were employed in Guiana since 1818 but on a large scale for the cultivation of cotton, sugar, clove, coffee, cinnamon, nutmeg and pepper between 1836 and 1840. In French Guiana, even before the abolition of African slavery in 1848, Fr. Louis Senegel had inquired into acquiring Indian labourers of a spice cultivator caste from the Malabar Coast, where spices were plenty, and to cultivate cinnamon and pepper in the forested hinterland. It had been mentioned that the French should bring to Guiana 1100 Indian farmers along with their wives and some also from Ceylon who were of the caste specially trained in cultivating cinnamon and preparing its precious bark. They desired to have farmers from the Malabar Coast and Sumatra who were used to cultivating pepper, to introduce it in Guiana. These two crops were felt important and judged which one among them the French should prefer too.[7] It must be mentioned in the outset that with the abolition of slavery the labour recruitment of coolies by the French for the sugar plantations developed. In France the abolition of slavery, spearheaded by Victor Schoelcher in his capacity as Under-Secretary of State for the Marine and the Colonies in 1848, was heralded as the triumph of liberty, equality and fraternity and as the inevitable consequence of French Republicanism ideology. He made serious efforts to abolish slavery and as a result on 27 April 1848 a decree was passed and slavery was abolished.

The System of Recruitment of Coolie Labour under the French East India Company

Indentured labour was valued less than slave labour in the French West Indies because its duration was less than a lifetime. However, the French in India had been asked to recruit labourers for cultivation in the American plantations and what they aimed was to have people from Mahe, Karaikal and Pondicherry. It was then decided to have an agency which could handle the affairs smoothly. Bedier took charge as French Governor of Pondicherry on 6 January 1851 and the Emigration Society of Pondicherry was established and it came into existence in the same year under the patronage of the French administration. It was felt significant to have the *maistry* (mestre derived from Portuguese meaning chief) as the superintendent of labourers while recruiting the workers in groups to be sent to French Guiana. It was also strongly felt the urgent need to have such intermediaries indispensable in order to have a good understanding between those who employed and the coolie labourers.[8] Two agencies were created while one functioned in Pondicherry under Chatelier de Souza and Venkatachalam Mudali to recruit workers. These Pondicherry agents recruited persons from Salem, South Arcot, Coimbatore and Mysore areas only. There was another agency for recruitment of coolies at Karaikal under Emile Hecquet and it recruited coolies from Thanjavur, Tiruchirapalli, Madurai and Tirunelveli areas only. The British Government of India through the Act of XIV of 1839 prohibited the desire and practice the French government to legalise the transport of coolies from British territories of Tamil Country in India. Further, according to the terms of the Act XV of 1842 it stopped the French for regulating the coolie migration to the Mauritius apprehending that it would be found impracticable to enforce wholesome conditions in the case of migration to French West India settlements like Guiana, Martinique and Guadeloupe.[9]

The Emigration Society of Pondicherry met the expenditure towards the preparation of the contract deed, making the passport for the individual, cost of medical checkup, his livelihood, maintenance or superintendence in the warehouse or place of stay and till boarding the ship. The rates were fixed on 25 April 1855. The amount for transporting the coolies for the American colonies was fixed at 42 rupees. Other than the Emigration Society, if work was undertaken by the concerned agents the amount fixed for sending a coolie to the American colonies, it was increased to three more rupees which was 45 rupees. As well known, the cost of migration was high because the migrants were too poor to pay this cost the employers bore the cost as an advance to the workers and tied the worker to the employer for a certain number of years. Typically a worker to the French West Indies was normally tied to an employer for a period of three years. A breach of contract could lead to arrest and prosecution. One particular arrangement that gained notoriety was Act 6 or the Special Act that gave the planters the right of private arrest prior to recourse to the legal system.

Sailing Voyages and Transport of Coolies from Pondicherry and Karaikal to French Guiana in South America

Ships sailed with the coolies recruited and it left Pondicherry and it touched first at Karaikal where coolies were again boarded the ships. Then it sailed and reached Mauritius. The third stopover was at Reunion and the ship crossed the Cape of Good Hope in Africa and proceeded to French Guiana in the mainland of South America.

Regarding the voyages it must be said that there was no proper and sufficient place and accommodation for the coolies in the ships. They had to stay at the bottom of the ship where rice, groundnut, bales of cloth and oil barrels were kept and stored. There was no proper light and ventilation. There was scarcity of food and drinking water. No proper medicine for the disease was available. Those who became sick and died were thrown into the sea. The condition of those travelled with children and kids had been deplorable and made like a hell. The British Government in India desired to know the French system of Indenture labour contract and so it deputed Franklin vide its communication dated 17 September 1857 to conduct an enquiry into the system of emigration from Pondicherry to the French West Indies. The honourable court vide its dispatch no. 50 of 29 July 1857 had directed the appointment of a gentleman conversant with the system of emigration in Madras Presidency for the purpose of ascertaining information of the Emigration Commissioners in Britain, by what means and under what circumstances it was found that results of the emigration from Pondicherry where apparently so much less attention was paid to the comfort of the emigrants, especially as regards the space allotted to each individual on board ship, can yet bear so favourable a comparison with the results of the emigration from Madras. Franklin's report of 21 January 1858 gave a very favourable view of the French arrangements.[10]

Brokers supplied persons to the registered bodies like the emigration society of Pondicherry and these middlemen received good brokerage. They kept the persons and delivered them to the captain of the ships and also received some good money. Then the ship's captain sold them to the owners of the plantations on arrival. Thus there were also persons who were illegally transported. French ships sailing to Guiana, Martinique Island and Guadeloupe Island with coolies had been found recorded with minute details in French documents. On 5 February 1853 a ship L'Aurelie sailed from Karaikal to Martinique with 322 emigrants.[11] The ship arrived finally with 313 passengers. Thus we are able to note the deaths of coolie passengers. The society of emigration that functioned in Pondicherry recruited persons during the times of famine in 1854 and it had exported 10,000 coolies from Pondicherry and Karaikal. Selon de Verninac, of the emigration society recruited 8000 coolies and they all hailed from the surroundings of Pondicherry.[12]

On 5 February 1853 a ship called Orley sailed from Karaikal to Martinique Island with 322 coolies. It reached Martinique Island extraordinarily and unusually after 15 months journey in the month of May 1854. Nine persons died on in the course of voyage. Others reached were half dead. On 8 September 1854 a report related to the ill treatment of some coolies of Tamil Country from British India on board the French ship Auguste in Karaikal was furnished to the British Government of India. The honourable court vide its judicial case no. 4 of 1855 brought out the same to the notice of the French Government which allowed the case which was said to be deplorable.[13]

Since 26 October 1854 coolies were shipped mainly through the supply of brokers who were approved. There was a severe famine and cholera that had spread in Pondicherry in 1854. People starved for food and at the height of famine caused by drought the French Governor Lalande de Calan expressed unorthodox views to a gathering of people who requested for supply of food. He very much liked and desired the people to migrate to American Colonies.[14]

In 1855, four ships left Pondicherry to Karaikal and proceeded to Guiana carrying coolies. The ship Le Arnaud, Le Hambourg, Le Bordeaux and L'Indien had carried 381 Tamils and they were taken to Martinique. The ships also sailed and had reached Guadeloupe with 437 Tamil coolies.[15] The ship Le Samuel Brown sailed away from Pondicherry with coolies and a surgeon was present on board to take care of the passengers who fell sick during the voyage. There was a broker called Vinayagam who had helped in the supply of coolie labourers for transport.

On arrival, the coolies were lodged in warehouses where they ate and slept. They were sent in batches to work in different sugar estates and farms.

After the expiry of contracts for a period of three years we find the re-departure of coolie migrants that took place between 1855 and 1861 which had been noted in documents. New arrival of coolies to Martinique Island and Guadeloupe Island had also continued from Pondicherry and in 1855 we find 2022 coolies were received from four ships Arnaud, Hambourg, Bordeaux and Indian. In the end of 1855, the total coolie immigrants had increased to 3704. The number of persons had swelled to 4496 by 31 December 1856.[16] Monsieur de Verninac was the then Governor of Pondicherry in 1856 and he reported vide his letter 24 December 1856 that 8 ships carried 3867 coolies to Martinique and four ships carried 1847 coolies to Guadeloupe and one ship to Guiana with 820 coolies.[17] The French had recruited 3250 coolies at Pondicherry and at Karaikal in 1858. 2525 coolies sailed and reached and the coolie population in total had further increased to 5775 coolies. Thus migrant coolies have been on the increase in due course of time.

The migration of coolies from Karaikal to the American colonies 1853-62

Year	*Number of coolie migrants*
1853	320
1854	318
1855	641
1856	355
1857	660
1858	1827
1859	1492
1860	1072
1861	1255
1862	243
Total	**8183**

Source: Roucaya Badat, *Un Comptoir français des Indes: Karaikal de 1850 a 1862*, Memoire de Maitrise, Universite de Aix-en-Provence, 1972, pp. 111-2.

French documents also mention the total number of coolie migrants both from Pondicherry and Karaikal together without splitting as they were of Tamil origin. Hence we find the combined or total statistics without individual mention of figures from the port of Pondicherry and Karaikal separately from 1857 to 1860.

The migration of coolies from Pondicherry to the American colonies, 1857-60

Year	*Number of coolie migrants*
1857	2481
1858	4495
1859	3667
1860	2547
Total	**13190**

Source: M. J. Mazard, *L'Immigration Indienne vers les colonies françaises, 1860-1880*, Memoire de Maitrise, Aix-en-Provence, 1972, p. 112.

Records of 1858 also provide the migration of coolies with details of sex including kids between the age of five and twelve and the number of children above the age of twelve years. These coolies from Pondicherry and Karaikal have been also put together in statistics. Hence we find the combined or total statistics of migrants to Martinique Island and Guadeloupe Island.

The migration of coolies from Pondicherry to the American colonies, 1858

Destination	*Men*	*Women*	*Infants*	*Children*	*Total*
Martinique	1651	255	64	62	2032
Guadeloupe	1976	352	47	88	2463

Source: Archives Nationales, Section Outre-Mer (hereafter ANSOM), Paris, Inde 466, Dossier 600, P.V. de la séance du 16 Octobre 1858 du conseil administration.

Migration of coolies continued and the ships from Pondicherry destined to Guiana had been mentioned in records in 1860. The total had been 2547 as furnished below.

The migration of coolies from Pondicherry to Guiana, 1860

Name of the ship	*Date/year*	*Coolies*
Richelieu	9 January 1860	494
Suger	6 April 1860	367
Reaumur	3 August 1860	520
Hampden	29 September 1860	514
Rubens	13 December 1860	652
Total		**2547**

Source: ANSOM, Inde 466, Dossier 600, letter of Ubraye of 10 Octobre 1860 of no. 497 and 23 Novembre 1860 of no. 502; ANSOM, Inde 466, Dossier 600, Etat Recapitulatif des engages embarques des Repenses, des recettes et des benefices faits par la Societe d' Emigartion suivant ses livres du 27 Juin 1859 au 23 Mai 1861.

Coolies recruited and transported by the agencies in Pondicherry and Karaikal to Guiana had been mentioned in records between 1861 and 1872. However, no ships sailed in 1862 1863, 1869, 1870 and 1871.

The migration of coolies from Pondicherry and Karaikal to Guiana, 1861-72

Date/year	*Coolie migrants*
1861	514
1864	275
1865	400
19 September 1865	413
1 December 1865	277
1866	392
1867	1116
1868	291
1872	398
Total	**4076**

Source: M. J. Mazard, *L'Immigration Indienne vers les colonies françaises*, p. 151; ANSOM, Inde, 467, Dossier 607, Tableau des immigrants Indieas introduits a la Martinique a la Guadeloupe et a la Guyane pendant les annees 1864 et 1846; ANSOM, Inde 468, Dossier 608, Etat des emigrants de L'Inde depuis le 1er Janvier 1866.

According to records we find 6551 Tamil speaking coolies who were agricultural workers, paddy cultivators, masons, shepherds, weavers and servants from villages and towns near Pondicherry and Karaikal mostly men and women between the age of 14 and 30 were cajoled with false promises of lucrative and hospitable work conditions or simply kidnapped onto French owned ships en route to Guiana between 1856 and 1877. As a result Tamils comprised a quarter of French Guiana's total population in due course of time.[18]

Books Printed in Pondicherry Sent in Ships to Guiana for the Use of Planters and for the Education of Tamil Coolie Children, 1865

Coolie Tamils in families sailed from Pondicherry and so it was found that printed books in Tamil and French were needed for the education of the children. It was also found useful to the French planters in Guiana. Hence the printed school text books were sent from Pondicherry to French Guiana. In 1865 a single shipment reached had become among the first collections of Tamil and French the bilingual books to be traded across the

French empire. Heeding to the request of Fr. Louis Savinien Dupuis the manger of the Catholic printing press in Pondicherry a book catalogue was forwarded to the four French Governors of Reunion, Martinique, Guadeloupe and Guiana. It was stated then by the Governor of Pondicherry in his letter to the Minister of the Navy and Colonies in Paris that overseeing Tamil indentured and coolie labourers would be very easy if the printed books were used by the French planters. The Tamil-French dictionary and grammar books had been highly appreciated for the use of the children and the planters. It also underlined the significance of easing the relations between plantation owners and the coolie workers as much as to guarantee the functioning of courts and tribunals too.[19] Of all the governors contacted, only the Governor of French Guiana responded favourably and he ordered 76 volumes of books, including dictionaries, grammars, workbooks, catechism, biblical stories and copies of Arabian Nights written or translated into Tamil from French and Latin.[20]

The French planters had employed interpreters who knew French and Tamil. They were also sent in ships to the American colonies. In a record dated 5 July 1860 we find a gentleman by name Sandou Rattinasami Udaiyar hailing from Pondicherry. He had been in Martinique Island for many years as an interpreter of Tamil language. It is reported that he was planning to visit Paris. His daughter the young girl was studying in the school and a boarder then in the convent of the Immaculate Heart of Mary in Pondicherry founded by Fr. Louis Savinien Dupuis. Interestingly we find that Sandou Rattinasami Udaiyar had sent two currency notes towards the expenditure and cost of meeting boarding and lodging for his daughter.[21] In fact in 1877 the British Raj outlawed Tamil migration to French Guiana when it became obvious that countless men, women and children had unnecessarily died of disease aboard ships and in plantations because the French had ignored the overseeing British government's requirement to hire Tamil–speaking interpreters to assist medical doctors.[22] Thus one can understand the profitability of coolie migration and the Tamil interpreters. Similar had been the case of those who returned but it has not been described in very different terms and contexts, but it seems that few migrants were able to accumulate sufficient capital to make any lasting improvement in their situation once they returned home. On the other hand, the migrants did regularly send their savings home to Pondicherry, creating a constant transfer of wealth which was fostered by the political integration of the French colonies. This mechanism made possible a significant redistribution of revenues, and productive reinvestments whose positive effect on Pondicherry and it had been difficult to assess. It must be said that the voyages from Pondicherry to Guiana were finally suspended in 1878.

Recruitment of Coolies from Pondicherry and Karaikal and Migration to Martinique Island in the Caribbean, 1853-79

There were some ships that left Pondicherry and touched at first Karaikal and after boarding of the coolies sailed then and reached Mauritius and the third stopover was at Reunion and after crossing the Cape of Good Hope proceeded to Martinique Island and coolies destined were allowed to land. Further the ships sailed then to Guadeloupe which was located still further. The coolies on arrival at Guadeloupe were sent to work in the sugar plantations. The French took great efforts to recruit coolies in Tamil country for it necessitated the labour needs of the empire in the Northern Atlantic islands.

Coolies recruited from Pondicherry and Karaikal to Martinique Island by the Society of Emigration in Pondicherry, 1853-60

Year	*Coolie migrants*
1853	327
1854	878
1855	381
1856	1546
1857	1227
1858	1534
1859	1891
1860	1078
Total	**8862**

Source: Victor Schoelcher, *Polemique Coloniale, 1882-1885*: *Suivi de Discourse et Articles Divers Fort-de-France*, 1979, vol. II, p. 224.

The French in Karaikal had posted agents to recruit coolies from Nagapattinam in British India and also at Tranquebar. On 17 April 1857 Hillary a French trader at Nagapattinam wrote to the British Government in India wherein he proposed that the migration of Tamil labourers from British ports should be permitted and he asked that he should have the exclusive privilege of engaging the workers for migration from the Madras Presidency. However the request was not approved.[23] Edward Robinson the ship having 300 tons sailed away from Pondicherry with coolies and those coolies who were ready for boarding were also taken in the ship at Tranquebar and the total number of coolies was 425 Tamils. Individual migrant coolies from Pondicherry to Martinique Island had been mentioned in documents in 1858 and 1859. The figures had increased and some times decreased owing to the tonnage of the ships which transported the coolies.

Coolie Migrants to Martinique Island, 1858-9

Date/year	*Ship name and tonnage*	*Coolie migrants*
27 January 1858	Nicolas Poussin, 445	455
9 June 1858	Reaumur, 555	569
24 August 1858	Richelieu, 514	539
November 1858	Nicolas Poussin, 445	445
1859	Siam	393
1859	Reaumur	525
23 January 1859	Paul Adrien	400
22 June 1859	Ville d' Agen	6302
2 August 1859	Siam	435
28 October 1859	Reamur	558
13 December 1859	Daubenton	386
Total		**5335**

Source: ANSOM, Inde 466, Dossier 600, Etat indiquant le nombre emigrants expedies aux Antilles du 1er Janvier 1858 au 21 Octobre suivant; ANSOM Inde 466, Dossier 600, Etat Recapitulatif des engages embarques des Repenses, des recettes et des benefices faits par la Societe d' Emigration suivant ses livres du 27 Juin 1859 au 23 Mai 1861.

Coolie migrants arrived in ships in Martinique Island had been mentioned from Pondicherry and Karaikal during 1861-1872. It is also found that no ships sailed in 1863 and 1864.

Migration of coolies from Pondicherry and Karaikal to Martinique Island, 1861-72

Year	*Coolie migrants*
1861	1109
1862	402
1865	403
1866	338
1867	2220
1868	937
1869	456
1870	937
1871	463
1872	788
Total	**8053**

Source: ANSOM, Inde 467, Dossier 607, Tableau des immigrants Indieas introduits a la Martinique a la Guadeloupe et a la Guyane pendant les annees 1864 et 1846; ANSOM, Inde 468, Dossier 608, Etat des emigrants de L'Inde depuis le 1er Janvier 1866; V. Schoelcher, *Polemique Coloniale 1882-1885*, vol. II, p. 224. Rapport de M.J. Beaujean sur le voyage de Richelieu transportant un convoy d' immigrants de Pondichery a la Martinique, *Revue Coloniale*, vol. III, 1860, p. 662.

On expiry of the period of contract, the coolies had returned to Pondicherry and Karaikal. If the living conditions were good perhaps they would not have returned and they would have certainly renewed. Therefore it is construed that Tamils who found safe living in Tamil country their motherland must have returned happily.

Repatriates of coolies from Martinique Island to Pondicherry and Karaikal, 1855-82

Year	*Coolie repatriates*
1855	1
1858	18
1859	68
1860	70
1861	245
1863	198
1864	276
1865	431
1867	286
1868	503
1871	25
1872	272
187	283
1874	162
1875	368
1879	502
1882	552
Total	**4, 260**

Source: Victor Schoelcher, Polemique Coloniale 1882-1885, Vol. II, p. 224.

It is also found in records that voyages from Pondicherry to Martinique Island were finally suspended in 1885. Hence coolie emigrants from Pondicherry also came to an end.

Coolies to Guadeloupe Island in the Caribbean from Pondicherry and Karaikal, 1854

Ships that sailed from Pondicherry also carried coolies destined for Guadeloupe Island. The contracts signed exclusive make mention of the place and the period in the deed in 1854. The emigration society of Pondicherry played a key role in the recruitment and migration of coolies from 1854 to 1860.

Coolie migrants from Pondicherry and Karaikal to Guadeloupe recruited by Society of Emigration in Pondicherry, 1854-60

Year	*Coolie migrants*
1854	314
1855	437
1856	1071
1857	1358
1858	1411
1859	1733
1860	808
Total	**7132**

Source: M. Singaravelou, *Les Indien de la Guadeloupe*, Thesis Bordeaux III, 1975, p. 50, see table. 1.

Some of the ships that sailed in 1858 and 1859 mention the tonnage of the ships and the number of coolie emigrants too. Such details are interesting to compare with the actual number of migrants who sailed in ships.

Migration of coolies to Guadeloupe Island from Pondicherry and Karaikal, 1858-59

Date/year	*Ship name and tonnage*	*Coolie migrants*
22 April 1858	Emile Pereire, 714	731
17 July 1858	Rubens, 719	738
November 1858	Hampden, 544	563
4 December 1858	Suger, 580	558
22 January 1859	Junon	220
25 June 1859	Jeune Albert	498
29 August 1859	Esperance	540
1859	Esperance	494
Total		**4342**

Source: ANSOM, Inde 466, Dossier 600, Etat indiquant le nombre emigrants expedies aux Antilles du 1er Janvier 1858 au 21 Octobre suivant; ANSOM Inde 466, Dossier 600 Etat Recapitulatif des engages embarques des Repenses, des recettes et des benefices faits par la Societe d' Emigration suivant ses livres du 27 Juin 1859 au 23 Mai 1861.

The ships that sailed also mention the various castes of the coolie migrants. It is found in a record of 1859 that as many as 481 migrants accompanied by the ships' surgeon Dr. Corre reached Guadeloupe. They were of various caste groups but mainly of artisans. The list mentions 97 persons under the category of others without any clue as to the caste and they were non-Tamils.

Migration of coolies and their castes to Guadeloupe Island, 1859

Caste	*Number of persons*
Agamudaiyars right hand caste	12
Ambattan right hand caste (barber-surgeon)	14
Barbers right hand caste	12
Idaiyars right hand caste	11
Kavarai chettis right hand caste	43
Muslims right hand caste	36
Oddars right hand caste	3
Raju right hand caste	1
Reddis right hand caste	11
Vellala right hand caste	44
Vannans right hand caste (washermen)	5
Kammalars left hand caste	6
Panchalattars left hand caste	74
Pulaiyars left hand caste	2
Pallis left hand caste	30
Pallar left hand caste	14
Vanniyars left hand caste	5
Sakkili left hand caste (cobblers)	3
Kallars	5
Chettis	5
Mahaffs	5
Fishermen	2
Cooks	2
Vadugars	7
Weavers	9
Thoetis (scavengers)	3
Melacarar (drum-beaters)	3

Source: M. Singaravelou, Les Indien de la Guadeloupe, pp. 20, 22, 28.

The number of coolie migrants sailing from Pondicherry and Karaikal to Guadeloupe in various ships sailed in the same year had been mentioned during 1859-65.

Coolie migrants from Pondicherry and Karaikal to Guadeloupe Island, 1859-65

Date/year	*Name of the ship*	*Coolie migrants*
1859	Daubenton	386
9 January 1860	Richelieu	494
6 April 1860	Suger	367
19 April 1860	Junon	361
29 September 1860	Hampden	514

(*Contd...*)

1861	Jacques Coeur	641
1861	Parmentier	503
25 February 1865	Daguerre	314
4 March 1865	Suger	325
12 March 1865	Jacques Coeur	462
Total		**4367**

Source: ANSOM Inde 466, Dossier 600, Etat Recapitulatif des engages embarques des Repenses, des recettes et des benefices faits par la Societe d' Emigartion suivant ses livres du 27 Juin 1859 au 23 Mai 1861; ANSOM, Inde 467, Dossier 607, Tableau des immigrants Indieas introduits a la Martinique a la Guadelopue et a la Guyane pendant les annees 1864 et 1846; ANSOM, Inde 468, Dossier 608, Etat des emigrants de L'Inde depuis le 1er Janvier 1866.

The number of coolie migrants sailing from Pondicherry and Karaikal to Guadeloupe swelled at times and also decreased during 1861-1872. The details had been furnished and the reasons are varied in nature such as droughts and famines.

Coolie migrants from Pondicherry and Karaikal to Guadeloupe, 1861-72

Year	*Coolie migrants*
1861	1939
1862	906
1863	1726
1864	636
1865	462
1866	1235
1867	3144
1868	1370
1869	915
1870	884
1871	935
1872	462
Total	**14614**

Source: M. Singaravelou, Les Indiens de la Guadeloupe, p. 50, see table 1; Rapport de M.A. Gaigneron sur le voyage suger transpotant un convoy d'immigrants de Pondichery a la Guadelopue, *Revue Coloniale*, vol. V, 1862, p. 712.

Return of Tamil Coolies from Guadeloupe to Pondicherry and Karaikal

On expiry of the contract for a period of three years, the coolie migrants returned in ships to Pondicherry. We find the details from 1854 to 1891. However we find gaps for many years in the records.

Repatriates of coolies from Guadeloupe to Pondicherry and Karaikal, 1854-91

Year	*Coolie repatriates*
1854	1
1861	65
1863	243
1865	297
1868	386
1871	344
1872	222
1873	1262
1877	305
1878	438
1882	508
1884	600
1885	958
1886	675
1887	808
1888	379
1889	830
1891	661
Total	**8982**

Source: M. Singaravelou, *Les Indiens de a Guadeloupe*, p. 50, see table 1.

While transporting the coolies in large numbers in ships, the French East India Company had appointed surgeons and physicians to attend to the medical needs and care of the coolie labourers. However, mortality of coolie labourers from the ships destined to American Colonies had been present and the details are recorded.

Mortality of coolie labourers from the ships destined to the American colonies

Year	*Ship name*	*Persons on board*	*Died during voyage*
1853	Aurelie	317	4
1854	Louis Napoleon	515	11
1854	Belle-Gabrielle	380	5
1854	Aurelie	320	6
1855	Arnaud	381	0
1855	Hambourg	443	6
1855	Bordeaux	576	12
1855	Indien	664	20
1856	Madagascar	822	15
1857	Richelieu	354	9
1857	Rubens	529	17
1857	Hampden	747	26
1857	Daubenton	570	21
1858	Indien	461	9
1858	Emile Pereire	729	20
1858	Richelieu	733	51
1858	Nicolas Poussin	530	17
1858	Richelieu	519	5
1858	Hampden	544	0
1858	Reaumer	559	15
1858	Rubens	738	9
1859	Suger	433	13
1859	Nicolas Poussin	469	5
1859	Paul Adrien	400	7
1859	Junon	220	4
1859	Ville de Agen	633	22
1859	Reaumur	558	9
1859	Richelieu	538	9
1859	Siam	429	7
1859	Esperance	541	2
1859	Reaumur	540	12
1860	Suger	397	3
1860	Parmentier	531	17
1860	Jacques Coeur	674	10
1860	Hampden	528	10
1860	Rubens	687	25
1861	Suger	412	11
1861	Siam	444	5
1861	Confiance	410	9
1861	Duguay-Trovin	536	20

(Contd...)

1861	Maurice et Reunion	388	30
1861	Jeune Albert	488	70
Total		**21687**	**578**

Source: ANSOM, Inde 467, Dossier 607, Releve des batiments qui ont transporte des Indiens dans nos colonies d' Amerique avant et depuis la convention, avec indication des mortalities survenues durant la traverse

Conclusion

The migration of Tamil indentured labourers to Guiana, Martinique and Guadeloupe under the French has been influenced by transatlantic slavery, but there were major differences between the terms of their origin and the form and evolution of the forms of servitudes in the Reunion and Mauritius Islands which were the only areas in the Indian Ocean where the French had developed plantation economy. But the development of plantation in the Northern Atlantic region of Guiana, Guadeloupe and Martinique had already acquired certain peculiar features of labour system that need to be distinguished. The terms used in the Atlantic system of slavery reveal an inherent animalization. The term *mulâtre* (and the English borrowed term mulatto) derives from the Portuguese and Spanish word *mulato*, which means mule an infertile offspring of interbreeding between a horse and a donkey. Similarly the term *câpresse or coffrees* comes from the Latin term *capra*, meaning goat. However, in Asia coolie in English was adopted referring to the wage-earner derived from Tamil term '*kuli/ coolie*' for an indenture labour. Thus there has been substantial variance in the regional specificities of naming labour in the world by the Europeans. It must be said at the outset that the Tamils in French Guiana, Martinique and Guadeloupe islands had to work in the plantations among the people of a multi-racial society.

It is evident from French records that the various types of people who migrated from Pondicherry and Karaikal to the French West Indies were those who suffered from poverty and starvation, those who were cheated by brokers, those who did not get jobs everyday, those who were evicted from the land, those who found non-employment and those who got job but no proper wages were paid. The droughts in Pondicherry during 1854, 1855, 1856, 1857, 1858, 1861, 1865, 1866, 1867, 1868, 1869, 1870, 1876 and 1877 perhaps accelerated the migration of the coolies. There was an increasing demand for sugar in the world, hence sugar plantations developed by the French in the West Indies necessitated immigration of coolies from Tamil country in French India. Though the price of sugar fell steeply in 1863 in the world market, the transportation of coolies from Pondicherry did not gradually fell. The total number of Tamil labourers in Guadeloupe

Island reached was 42,326 from 1854 to 1889. Similarly Tamils reached in Martinique Island were 25,509 from 1854 to 1889. The percentage of death of coolies transported was between 7 per cent minimum to 14 per cent maximum. Labour migration was controlled by numerous limiting regulations and the French in Pondicherry rose to the pressure of demand from French planters in the West Indies.

It must be also pointed out that the observation made by a British official in 1859 is revealing in connection with the migration. He noted prices of commodities and the cultivated area around Pondicherry and in general the South Arcot district for 20 years and recorded that agricultural yields per acre had very much declined between 1800 and 1860.[24] Therefore many agricultural labourers in South Arcot areas had moved over to Pondicherry from where there was possibility for overseas migration under the French in the sugar plantations in the American colonies. The well existed networks between Pondicherry and French West Indies accelerated coolie migration by reducing obstacles. It also led to uprooting labour from India and planting in West Indies for those Tamils who were newly job-hunting in the overseas. This helped on a large scale in the strengthening of the labour recruitment system which supplanted contract-recruitment or indentured labour.

Notes

1. Frances Armytage, *The Free Port System in the British West Indies: A Study in Commercial Policy, 1766-1822*, London, 1953, pp. 10-11, 55.
2. Arthur Redford and Brian W. Clapp, *Manchester Merchants and Foreign Trade, 1794-1858*, Manchester, 1934, p. 3.
3. Dale W. Tomich, *Slavery in the Circuit of Sugar: Martinique and the World Economy, 1830-1848*, Johns Hopkins University Press, Baltimore, 1990, pp. 54-6.
4. Philip D. Curtin, *The Atlantic Slave Trade: A Census*. Madison: University of Wisconsin Press, Madison, 1969, pp. 78, 84.
5. Eric E. Williams, *From Columbus to Castro: The History of the Caribbean 1492-1969*, London, 1970, pp. 325-6.
6. Louis-Napoléon Bonaporte, *Analyse de la Question des Sucres*, Administration de Librairie, Paris, 1842, p. 10.
7. Centre des Archives de Outre-Mer (hereafter CAOM), Aix-en-Provence, Guyane 1819, Extraite d' une letter ecrite de Fr Louis Senegel en date du 12 Avril 1819 a son excellence, la Ministre de la Marine, par M. Mahe, capitaine de vaisseau, introduction d' Indiens a la Guiane francaise, 1818-1822.
8. Archives Nationales, Section Outre-Mer (hereafter ANSOM), Paris, Inde 464, Dossier 590, Letter of Governor Bedier to Ministry dated 23 May 1851.

9. V. Lalitha, 'Emigration of British Subjects from French Ports in India to French Colonies-Proposal to Legalise – Papers Relating to Down to 1858', *Revue Historique de Pondichery*, no. XIII, 1976 - 80, pp. 162-168, see pp 162-3.
10. Ibid., p. 168.
11. ANSOM, Paris, Inde 465, Dossier 594, Letter of Minister to de Verninac dated 23 April 1853.
12. ANSOM, Inde 465, Dossier 595, Letter of Verninac to Minister dated 18 July 1855.
13. V. Lalitha, Emigration of British Subjects, p. 166.
14. Adrien Launay, *Histoire des Missions de L'Inde: Pondichery, Maissour, Coimbatour*, 4 vols., Paris, 1895-1898, vol. III, p. 103.
15. Singaravelou, *Les Indien de la Guadeloupe*, Thesis Bordeaux III, 1975, p. 50, see table 1.
16. ANSOM, Inde 465, Dossier 599, Ministerial dispatch of 23 January 1857.
17. V. Lalitha, Emigration of British Subjects, p. 167.
18. Singaravelou, *Les Indiens de la Caraibe*, III vols., Paris, 1987.
19. CAOM, Aix-en-Provence, Inde 1863, Envoie du catalogue des ouvrages en langue tamoule edites par l'Imprimerie de la mission, see the letter from the Governor to Minister of the Marine and Colonies, written from Pondichery dated 18 February 1863, Circulire addressee aux colonies et relative a une souscription a des ouvrages en langue tamoule edites par l'Imprimerie de la mission Catholique en Inde, 1863-1865.
20. Sonia N. Das, *Linguistic Rivalries: Tamil Migrants and Anglo-French Conflicts*, Oxford, 2016.
21. S. Jeyaseela Stephen, ed., *The Hearbeat of a Missionary: Letters and Reports of Louis Savinien Dupuis in Pondicherry, 1839-74*, Pondicherry, 2017, document no. 30, p. 71.
22. CAOM, Aix-en-Provence, Guyane 1862, Process–verbaux de la Commission instiutee par decisison du Gouverneur en date du 28 Janvier 1862, a l'effet de proceder a une enquete sur l'etat moral et sanitaire des immigrants indiens introduite dans la colonie par le navire Le Parmentier' Convoi du Parmentier, partie de Pondichery 25 Mars 1861 arrive a Cayenne 9 Juillet 1861.
23. V. Lalitha, Emigration of British Subjects, p. 167.
24. R. Ratnam, *Agricultural Development in Madras State Prior to 1900*, Madras, 1966, p. 25.

Chapter - 4

Immigration of Tamils from Madras and the Indentured Labour Contracts for Mauritius: Understanding the Lived and Remembered Lives of the Migrants, 1829-90

Cornwallis who became the Governor-General of India in 1786 noticed that slaves were transported on a large scale from Bengal. Hence vide his proclamation dated 22 July 1789 he banned the slave exports from the Bengal Presidency.[1] This step taken led to follow the same idea of banning slave exports in the Madras Presidency also vide an order issued on 8 March 1790.[2] Since the early 1790s the British authorities took various steps to prevent children in particular from being sold into slavery and to impede the exportation of slaves from their British-Indian territories. In Tamil Country, some districts like Thanjavur and Tirunelveli had continued to function as slave trading centers as late as in 1812 and so it attracted the attention of the British officials. These areas had continued to remain very important for slave trading even by 1819-20.[3] C. M. Lushington the district collector of Tiruchirapalli in his letter dated 1 July 1819 reported that the *pallars* were usually sold with the land in which they worked, and they were also very frequently sold independently of the land in question.[4] J. Vaughan the English Company official in his letter to the Board of Revenue in Madras dated 20 July 1819 noted the indiscriminate sale of men, women and children in Tamil country and he pointed out that the local slaves were frequently transferred from one owner to another by sale, mortgage or hire.[5] Kidnapping and the sale of children as slaves were commonly found noticed in Thanjavur and Tirunelveli in 1825 which had become a nuisance.[6] Slave trading had also further continued even during the early 1830s.[7] This type of kidnapping activities of the children from the territory of the English East India Company and selling and exportation of the slaves to the French settlements of Pondicherry and Karaikal became a severe headache and a big problem of much concern for the British.

In Britain, slavery was abolished in 1831 and a law was passed in the parliament in 1833 and it came into force. As a result slavery was also abolished in British India in 1843. After the abolition of slavery in the British Empire, it is estimated that Mauritius had received approximately 455,000 labourers from various parts of India.[8] Persons immigrated from the port of Madras between 1852 and 1858 included largely from Ganjam, Rajamundhry, Vishakapattinam, Samalcotta and Nellore. This trend of Telugus migration continued even after 1861.[9] The British in Mauritius in 1865 had sent envoys to Madras for the recruitment of labourers.[10] It is important and necessary to differentiate the various ethnic group of migrants from India like Uttar Pradesh, Bihar and from Eastern India like the Bengalis and the Oriyas who sailed in ships from the port of Calcutta. Further from the colonial records we find mention of migration of South Indians in general terms and these migrants were notably Kannadigas from Mysore areas, Telugus from Cudappah Kurnool and other areas of coastal Andhra and Tamils who sailed in ships from the port of Madras. The recruitment details of all these labourers have been put for the sake of convenience of the British administrators in the records of Madras presidency. It must be pointed out here the Madras Presidency itself was one that covered Bellary in Karnataka and Guntur in Andhra having mixed group of people having different languages of origin. Hence I wish to neatly differentiate and concentrate only on the migrants of Tamil speaking areas because this immigrant group had an identity, name, number and a story to tell as they hailed from a separate cultural milieu of world and a distinct language totally different from all others.

The lived experiences of the Tamil migrants and the geographical origins of the labourers within the Tamil country itself is important to be examined which had not caught the attention of historians, sociologists and anthropologists. Hence it is high time and very necessary in exploring the micro-history. The traditional Tamil social historiography of the ancient and medieval periods cannot be understood in the same vein of the modern world for the Tamil society had made a complete break from the past after the advent of the Europeans where remarkable social progress had been made. Hence we should aim to focus on the human agency, irrespective of castes and communities in Tamil country to study the world view of the wage earners under indenture which was not life-long slavery that developed in the modern age. Resistance of indentured workers against an inhumane system of labour and exploitation had also developed in the colonial age. We would be therefore able to know better the functioning of the inner and the outer world of the Tamils in general and the indentured immigrants in particular during the age of global contact.

The Indentured Labour Immigrants from Madras, Pondicherry and Tranquebar to Mauritius, 1829-38

Mauritius came under the British administration and between August and October 1829 more than 1,500 Indian (besides Chinese) indentured labourers were introduced. They had mainly come from the port cities of Madras, Calcutta and Singapore. Gaillardon Company, a local Mauritian enterprise, played a key role in their importation of labourers.[11] In October 1829, John Finiss in his communication mentioned to Colonel Barry, the Chief Secretary to Government in Port Louis, that it was his duty to state the immigration circumstances are very favourable at the outset and that if the experiment succeeded, further importations of labourers would no doubt take place.[12] The law enforcement officer of Mauritius in 1829 had also referred to the importation of hundreds of indentured labourers to work on the island's sugar estates and he said it as an experiment being carried out by the Mauritian planters.[13]

The Franco-Mauritian sugar estate owners mistreated their workers. In addition, they either paid wages late or did not pay them at all. The planters had not fulfilled their other contractual obligations to their workers. Several labourers therefore had said that they had been highly deceived by the labour recruiters who had promised that they would get good wages and they had to do only light work. In spite of the major grievances, the Tamil indentured workers lived and worked in 1829 for several weeks on some of the island's large sugar estates. The labourers mentioned that they were miserably misled by the recruiters in Pondicherry and Karaikal with regard to the type of employment in which they would be engaged in Mauritius.[14] Over a period of time, the indentured workers therefore refused to work, deserted the sugar estates. They were arrested as vagrants and resorted to petty crimes in Port Louis, the colony's administrative headquarters.[15] This became a major concern for the British colonial authorities in Mauritius and the police force. Between December 1829 and May 1830, the authorities tried their best to sort out the problem and silently sent away the majority of the indentured workers in ships to Madras.

According to immigration records preserved in Mauritius, Lotah born in 1804 (immigrant no. 3158) had arrived in Mauritius from Madras in June 1834 when he was 30 years old. He came to work for Mr. Hardy, part owner of Argy sugar estate in the district of Flacq in the eastern part of the island of Mauritius, on a five year contract as a labourer. Earlier Lotah had left his native village to work in Madras when he was a young boy.[16] After working for Hardy for more than two years, Lotah ran away in August 1836 from Argy sugar estate to Port Louis where he worked as a porter for several days. Later he was arrested as a vagrant and he was sentenced by Charles Anderson the Special Magistrate to serve seven days at hard labour by breaking stones in the work yard of the Bagne prison. Before being sentenced, Lotah informed the magistrate that he had run away because he was unable to endure the difficult living and working conditions in the estate and his wage was not paid on time and always received late. His complaint was just dismissed. Mr. Hardy the owner of the estate had requested the Magistrate to return Lotah to his sugar estate after the punishment period.[17] By 1839, Lotah had remained and served his term of contract without any untoward incident and in 1840 he petitioned the British governor to remain in Mauritius and continued to work and live on the same sugar estate.[18] Thus we find cases of some who preferred to stay and not to return to Tamil country over a period of time.

Since slavery was abolished by the British in Mauritius in 1834, the early immigrants to Mauritius after 1834 were the wage labourers or coolies i.e., indentured labourers. The French and British planters in Mauritius were in need of workers and so they asked for supply from Tamil country. The French administration made arrangements and it also recruited coolies from Tranquebar and the ships sailed to Mauritius. According to English records, we find that on 22 March 1837 F. Dick the colonial secretary of Mauritius wrote a letter to the Secretary of Madras government in which he demanded to restrain a ship sailing from the port of Pondicherry and taking coolies from Tranquebar. The ship Edward Robinson of 300 tons had a registered burden of having on a late voyage from Pondicherry and Tranquebar therefore arrived in Mauritius with 425 coolies from Tamil country, and all of them were under agreements to serve as labourers or domestic servants. The Governor of Mauritius had deemed it necessary to give intimation to the captain of that vessel that he should, in future should bring only the coolies not of any number beyond what was allowed. If happened so the ship would not be allowed to land at Port Louis in Mauritius. The same ship was about to return to Pondicherry on a similar voyage and it being most desirable to the interest of humanity that every proper restraint should be placed upon the captain of vessels in regard to the number of passengers they may receive on board. The colonial secretary of Mauritius said that he had informed the governor's reactions so that he would move the Governor in Council of Madras to make such communication to the French Government of Pondicherry to attend to the problem and also to ensure to provide proper medical care to coolies. He stated that there was no surgeon on board the ship Edward Robinson and there was no person capable of giving medical assistance to coolies in case of sickness or an accident occurring.[19] According to records of 1838 we find *pallar* labourers migrated from Tamil country and they had signed contracts and reached Mauritius.[20] The system of indentured labour had been questioned in Parliament in Britain in 1837 and denounced by Thomas Fowell Buxton and Lord Brougham. The government of India thereafter in 1838 ordered a ban on further coolie shipments.

Living Conditions of the Tamil Coolie Immigrants in Mauritius

It has been reported and well painted about the living conditions of the Tamil labourers by James Backhouse who visited Port Louis between March and May 1838. He mentioned that after the passing of act abolishing slavery, an arrangement was sanctioned by the British Colonial Government, for the introduction of a large number of Tamil and Indian labourers into Mauritius. They were engaged at five rupees (equal to ten shillings), a month as pay for five years also with necessary items such as one pound and three quarters of rice, a quarter pound of red-gram, and one ounce of ghee, or butter daily. But for every day, they were absent from their work, they were to return to work for two days to their masters, who retained one rupee per month, and to repay the advance made of six months' wages, and to defray the expenses of their passage. James Backhouse also added that if these coolie labourers came to Port Louis to complain about their masters, they were lodged in the Bagne prison, till their masters were summoned. The estate owners had a great advantage before the magistrate, over their servants. The coolies being foreigners, but few of them could speak French, and they had none to assist them in pleading their case. They universally represented themselves as having been deceived with respect to the kind of labour to be extracted of them.[21]

During 1839 and 1844, apart from the poor working and living conditions and ill treatment of the Tamil workers on the sugar estates, the double-cut system was another important reason why the early Tamil workers escaped from the sugar estates and ran away from their employers.

This fact has been reported by James Backhouse, a British Quaker missionary to Mauritius, and also confirmed by Thomas Joseph Hugon (also known as Thomy Hugon) a Franco-Mauritian colonial official who became the Second Protector of Immigrants.[22]

In February 1839, *Le Mauricien*, a local pro-planter newspaper, reported that Tamils and other Indians employed as caterers and artisans were well paid and their number was gradually increasing. Many indentured workers who worked and lived in Port Louis probably also encouraged by their fellow men working in sugar plantations in the rural to come and seek better opportunities at Port Louis the colony's economic centre.[23] The city provided jobs easily where they could work as dockworkers, caterers, boatmen, domestic servants, messengers and a handful among them were masons, carpenters and blacksmiths.

Tamil Labour Recruitment and Shipping Coolies from Madras to Mauritius, 1842-80

Owing to the problems faced emigration was banned in Mauritius between 1839 and 1842. In 1839 the apprenticeship system ended on 1 April 1839 and it signalled the emancipation of slaves. The ban on emigration was lifted in 1842. The India Act XV of 1842 regulated the emigration to Mauritius of those Indians who came under the jurisdiction of the English East India Company. It provided for a Protector of Immigrants in Mauritius and gave the colonial government the option of appointing a second Protector. Emigration was permitted from Madras where there were to be Emigration Agents, acting for the Mauritius government but answerable to the Presidency governments. By providing such Protectors and Agents it was hoped that the Indian labourers would receive ample protection on the outward and return voyages and during their stay in the colonies. The first ship Emerald Isle cleared from Calcutta under this system arrived at Port Louis on 23 January 1843. The planters were reluctant to employ female immigrants from Bengal who simply followed the men to whom they were attached. Under the India Act XXI of 1843 the ban on emigration to the several colonies was lifted but for the time being emigration was confined to Calcutta. In 1844 the British Government took emigration in its own hands due to abuses in the system.

Madras subsequently became a centre of emigration to Mauritius. Captain Christopher Bidon the protector in Madras reported that main flow of coolie recruits came from the overpopulated Tamil districts where the landless labourers had a hopeless struggle for survival. The untouchables numbered though in some districts more numerous, and they formed in Chingleput district 27 per cent of the population and in Thanjavur district 21 per cent. Bidon reported that the majority of his recruits came from Thanjavur and Tiruchirapalli and South Arcot districts.[24]

Labour recruitment in Tamil country and migration to Mauritius is evident from an account and the deposition of Muthusamy, an inhabitant of Natham, a village in the district of Tiruchirapalli. It is highly revealing and depicts the pressures that commonly bore upon small peasant cultivators and the manners in which they landed at ports for emigration. Muthusamy affirmed that he was cultivating the land of his maternal uncle Kamatchi Naathan in the village of Natham for several years. But the produce after payment of the tax to the British Government proved insufficient for the support and maintenance of his family and children. Consequently he left his village in 1842 with the intention of earning his livelihood at Madras. On his way he heard that labourers for Mauritius were obtaining service at Pondicherry through the means of one Karuppayee. On his applying to her, she took Muthusamy and 29 other men to a French Gentleman who carried them to the police office, where their names were registered and they then signed a document expressing their desire to proceed to Mauritius to serve under Mr. Cochin for five years, on a salary of 5 Rupees each per month as well as batta (allowances) and clothes. They received each of them three months wages in advance. They embarked in ships with 170 others in a vessel bound for Mauritius, where they arrived after a voyage of 33 days. On landing Mr. Cochin got their names registered at the police office and employed them to work in the sugarcane plantation.[25]

Recruitment of people for overseas migration during 1841 especially in the early years had been very significant to note. Many were found outside the bondage of debt and serfdom.[26] The statement of immigrants like Venkatachalam, Arunachalam and Vaithilinga Nayakkar during the course of examination while boarding the ship Marie Laure on 7 May 1841 is revealing.[27] Owing to demand, the migrants were recruited in 1857 during religious festivals and large social gatherings. These details are found mention in the deposition of people when sailed to Mauritius.[28] Further, Muthusamy Pillai stated that he was recruited at Keevalore during the visit to Nagore where he attended the *kanduri* festival.[29]

Recruits in 1843 were requested to wear identification tags to prevent substitutes and to avoid the increasing frauds that took place. The British desired to mark the migrants and did on the thumb nail.[30] Later all emigrants had tin or tape badges affixed to their wrists and arms secured with sealing wax.

The wages advanced to recruits at Madras in 1843 was 2 ½ rupees per month and the sum for six months with a total of rupees 15 was paid. Pothan was to be advanced funds in 1843 to bring his family and friends to Mauritius. Returnee recruiters were also active in Madras as the case of Ramasamy from Madurai area was interested to bring his relatives and friends to Mauritius.[31]

Under the recruitment system tenders for the supply of emigrants were initiated in 1850 from the local merchants and agents who advanced money to supervisors to choose and collect recruits from two miles area to 300 miles inland. They were supposed to maintain the emigrants until the embarkation.[32] Subramania Pillai and others were employed by the contractors. Swamy *maistry* had worked for Venkata Subburayan and he reported that the latter kept and maintained two different accounts books while one was a true one and the other a false one.[33] Muthusami Pillai had placed a signboard in front of his house in 1866 inviting emigrants who wished to go over to Mauritius. When his Mauritius license had expired he held a licence to recruit coolies for Ceylon.[34]

Male immigrants were bound to work for a specified time and employer, under threat of penal sanctions in case of default, according to a type of contract, known as an indenture. Though males were largely transported in ships the first indentured women were taken to Mauritius by private importers at a time when slaves were being released from a lifetime of bondage on the plantations and in the homes of colonists. Most women immigrants were employed on verbal or short-term agreements, or undertook domestic service and other home-based labour in 1843. Migration which was placed under British government controls was henceforth aimed to regulate every aspect of the lives of Tamils and Indians under indenture.[35] It has been pointed out that the implementation of sex ratios ensured that overall around 40 women emigrated for every 100 men during the operation of government-regulated indentured migration from India between 1843 and 1890.[36]

The form of agreement for intending emigrants contains necessary particulars of the emigrant executing a contract for service in the colony of Mauritius. The details include registration date, number, name of the emigrant, dependants, relation, sex, age, caste, religion, name of the father, residence, name of the district, village or town, religion, occupation and finally with the mention that the emigrant agrees to emigrate on the conditions of service specified on the reverse, with specific mention of 'executed in my presence and his x mark of emigrant'. We find also the name of Registering Officer, with date and place. There is a note added saying that this form is to be filled up in the Office of the Registering officer in English in triplicate. The fitness of the Civil Surgeon of the place had been also recorded.

Medical examination of female recruits by European doctors and other emigration officials was vociferously objected to by their partners and resisted. In Karaikal the female recruits had refused to submit to the standard medical examination before embarkation.[37] A register of ship load of migrants in 1843 who were dealt with had noted their castes and districts in Tamil country. However, it may be mentioned that most of the registers until 1865 do not record particulars of the castes of the emigrants.

Immigration of Males in a Voyage in 1843 by District-wise from Tamil Country to Mauritius

District name	*Emigrants*
Madras	27
Chingleput	5
Cuddalore	20
Thanjavur	98
Tiruchirapalli	80
Madurai	13
Others	9
Total	**252**

Source: Mahatma Gandhi Institute, Moka, Mauritius, P.E. Series, Ship Arrivals and Distribution List of Indentures Labourers, Indian Immigration Register, 1843

Caste Identification of the Male Immigrants in 1843 from Madras to Mauritius

Caste name	*Numbers*
Paraiyars	40
Pulayars	32
Padayachi	26
Vellala	24
Ambattan	14
Kallars	14
Pallans	10
Others	92
Total	**252**

Source: Mahatma Gandhi Institute, Moka, Mauritius, P.E. Series, Ship Arrivals and Distribution List of Indentures Labourers, Indian Immigration Register, 1843.

The bounty system of labour recruitment was abolished based on the recommendation of Anderson the Special Magistrate in Mauritius. Thereafter a new system known as the contingent system was introduced in 1844. This contingent system had established a fixed quota of immigrants to be brought in monthly and a stricter selection in the quality of those labourers chosen. Although Anderson had recommended for 500 coolies only be brought monthly, this figure was considered too insufficient owing to labour demand in the plantations. The port of Madras was reopened as a place to allow for an embarkation of 3000 additional. The main aim in increasing the coolie labour supply was also to depress the wages. It was felt that 7 rupees per month instead of five rupees fixed earlier was considered too high as wages for the coolies in 1842.[38] In the year 1843 we find that 15,125 coolie men, 1830 women and 548 children had arrived in many ships that sailed from Madras to Mauritius. Thus a total of 17,503 emigrants reached in a year.

It has been followed by 1852 in Mauritius that the coolie could land as a free man, and he was at liberty to conclude with the planters such a contract as he pleased. The emigration agent had reported this matter on 20 September 1852.[39] Thus there had been a change in the policy and system followed in labour recruitment. The free return passage by the immigrants was also cancelled. The abolition of free return passage from Mauritius in 1853 had led to the rise of proportion of women among the emigrants to 25 per cent.[40] Added to this provision was also made for the celebration of marriages in Mauritius according to Tamil customs in 1853 whom they may not have considered to be a genuine husband. Conversely, women who migrated as co-wives might find that their polygamous marriage was not recognized, which meant, of course, that if a second wife left her husband, neither she nor her abductor could be prosecuted, because the first wife alone was considered the legal spouse.[41]

Large scale migrations took place from Madras, Chingleput South Arcot, Thanjavur and Tiruchirapalli districts. The protector of emigrants in Madras wrote on 9 May 1854 that these districts in Tamil country would be in a state of agrarian crisis to the absence of the cultivating class.[42] Under Governor Higgison private immigration was once again restored in 1855. Emigration to Mauritius was suspended in 1856 following eighty-one deaths among a shipload of Indians abandoned on an island off the north coast of Mauritius. A by-product of this incident was the Indian Act XIX of 1856, empowering the Governor-General to suspend emigration to any territory where he had cause to believe that conditions for the Indians were unsatisfactory.

The protector of emigrants in Madras reported in 1857 that Thanjavur and Tiruchirapalli became the main coolie recruiting and emigration districts while formerly the districts of Madras and Chingleput had remained active. The emigrants from Madras were chiefly *paraiyars* with considerable number of *sudras* and few Muslims.[43] The contingency system was again replaced in 1858 by a contract system in Mauritius. This system ended the freedom of the labour to choose an employer after his arrival in Mauritius. They were to sign a contract in Madras itself binding them to the employer for a period of three years.[44] Contractors were engaged and they helped in labour recruitment in Madras. There was no depot for emigrants to Mauritius in Madras until 1859, and the coolies recruited came to be lodged thereafter in contractor's godowns.[45] There had been decent profit well acquired by those contractors who were involved in the transportation of coolie emigrants.

Having acquired capital in the work in Mauritius some Indians had gone to the extent of functioning as independent proprietors, job contractors and shop owners. As they moved into the colonial elite, they became in turn employers, and occasionally exploiters of Tamil labourers. It is reported that Kaali Muthu had migrated from Tranquebar as a boy in 1859. He was employed by Dilip for five years, and then in 1864 went to work for Gungah, an Indian jeweller. Being then arrested as a deserter from Dilip's employ, he was forced to enter a new three year contact with Dilip in order to avoid imprisonment and separation from his pregnant wife. Thus we notice the status and position of Dilip is to that of a local European employer, and at his shop and residence, he often played host to the British magistrate of the district, and he was also thus hand in glove with the local judiciary in Mauritius.[46]

Classification of Immigrant Coolies from Madras to Mauritius, 1850-61

Year	*Men*	*Women*	*Children*	*Total*
1850	2729	608	299	3636
1851	2804	712	499	4015
1852	3854	826	686	5366
1853	3146	798	581	4525
1854	4593	1357	1364	7314
1855	4068	1426	1234	6728
1856	3014	1046	876	4936
1857	2772	985	878	4635
1858	7240	2742	2106	12088

(*Contd...*)

1859	6319	2543	2172	11034
1860	2519	1126	670	4315
1861	3107	1153	814	5074
Total	**46,165**	**15,322**	**12,179**	**73666**

Source: BL, House of Parliamentary Papers, Report on coolie emigration from India, Table A, The number of men, women and children emigration to Mauritius from Madras from 1842 to 1870, pp. 72-73.

The period between 1860 and 1880 in Mauritius witnessed the gradual decline of the importance of indentured Tamil immigration. Social and economic transition took place in colonial Mauritius which saw the end of the Mauritian sugar boom or revolution, the centralization of the sugar industry, the disappearance of many important sugar estates, and a restructuring of the Mauritian economy. In 1865 W.H Marsh the Assistant Colonial Secretary was sent to India. He listened to the lamentations of the agent in Madras who complained that although he had engaged a contract to provide 2000 recruits at a commission for 9 rupees per head the man had produced only 500, who were willing to go to Mauritius. Labourers in Tamil country were attracted to other join in the works of building railways and to the coffee plantations in Nilgiris.[47]

Classification of Immigrant Coolies from Madras to Mauritius, 1862-70

Year	*Men*	*Women*	*Children*	*Total*
1862	2949	1032	779	4760
1863	1684	690	646	3020
1864	1265	852	396	2513
1865	1709	858	743	3310
1866	1484	759	828	3071
1868	215	84	59	358
1869	820	309	159	1288
1870	814	330	192	1336
Total	**10940**	**4914**	**3802**	**19,656**

Source: BL, House of Parliamentary Papers, Report on coolie emigration from India, Table A, The number of men, women and children emigration to Mauritius from Madras from 1842 to 1870, p. 74.

The protectors of immigrants in Mauritius did not exercise and conduct any inspection of the coolies in the sugar plantations by 1868. The housing facilities and the treatment of the labourers were bad. The laws were effectively evaded and subverted. This was in large part the result of the official prejudice being highly in favour of the planters.[48] Working conditions in the plantations in Mauritius were since deplorable people deserted their employers. Nagan and Kamatchi's 14 years old son was given two years punishment in prison for running away from his employer in 1868. Some had indulged in petty crimes while salary remained unpaid for long. Ramalingam and Alamelu's son was sent away for five years, for a petty theft.[49] Thus we find removal of indentured children from parental care. The offender minors were taken into government-run reformatories which had been developed by the British in Mauritius.

Regional Indentured Labour Immigrants from Tamil Country to Mauritius, 1869-73

District name	*Males*	*Females*	*Total*
Madras	34	17	51
Chingelput	153	44	197
North Arcot/Chittoor	150	55	205
South Arcot/Cuddalore	40	10	50
Thanjavur	123	86	209
Tiruchirapalli	37	16	53
Total	**537**	**228**	**765**

Source: Mahatma Gandhi Institute, Moka, Mauritius, P.E. Series, Ship Arrivals and Distribution List of Indentures Labourers, Indian Immigration Register, 1869-73

Caste-wise Identification of Tamil Coolie Immigrants from Madras to Mauritius, 1869-73

Caste name	*Males*	*Females*	*Total*
Paraiyars	116	52	168
Reddiyars	93	45	138
Vanniyar	88	34	122
Vellalars	81	39	120
Kaikolar weavers	29	8	37
Saliyar weavers	24	16	40
Muchiyars	44	12	56
Others	54	30	84
Total	**529**	**236**	**765**

Source: Mahatma Gandhi Institute, Moka, Mauritius, P.E. Series, Ship Arrivals and Distribution List of Indentures Labourers, Indian Immigration Register, 1869-73

The coolie emigration of males from Madras to Mauritius was 72,230 between 1842 and 1870. The number of females in the same period was 22,066 and the children had been 16,529. Thus we find a total of 1, 10, 825 emigrants.[50] Migration to Mauritius had drained off several thousand Tamils. During the two decades of 1850-1870 the streams of migration was huge and the Tamils had migrated from Madras.

Coolie Immigrants from Madras to Mauritius, 1875-80

Year	*Coolie emigrants*
1875	2507
1876	2558
1877	2844
1878	3647
1879	6548
1880	3192
Total	**21, 296**

Source: Report on moral and material condition of India, 1880-1, p. 87

Asylums and Orphanages: Institutional Developments and the Indentured Labour in Mauritius, 1885-89

According to records, most elderly women in Mauritius were sent home for being invalids. They were removed from the colony in 1885 so as to avoid being a burden and charge on the public treasury. Some women had successfully managed the colonial authorities. They avoided admittance to the asylum an institution for the poor that came to function. Adaikalam, the woman whose fingers were paralyzed, refused to get admitted and enter into an asylum. She also failed to give up her child to an orphanage. Hence she had to face difficulties when refused rice rations from the Poor Law Commissioner in Mauritius. She was then registered for deportation to Madras and asked a free return passage. Facing a forced departure, she somehow arranged and hastily produced a provider.[51]

Under indenture it was considered a reason good enough to consign their offspring to government orphanages which were set up in Mauritius. Immoral behavior by a Tamil women and the fate of the children had been reported. Rammiya Seenaa had applied for the discharge of her three small children, Julie, Edith and Augusta from the orphanage in Mauritius. At that time her conduct was investigated by Mrs. Wilkinson of the local Girls' School. This lady learnt and reported after ascertaining the truth that Rammiya's legal husband was the father of Augusta and that of Edith the middle daughter was the offspring of a Frenchman then in Bourbon (Reunion Island). Nothing certain was known as to the father of Julie. Therefore Mrs. Wilkinson stated that, Thiruvengadam, the husband of Rammiya had left her 14 or 15 years ago. It happened because of her immoral conduct. Thiruvengadam declared that if the children were all registered in his name he did not want them given away to their mother. Hence it was mentioned that the children would not be safe and they should be not discharged from the orphanage. Thus Thiruvengadam's testimony had sealed the fate of the children.[52]

The Return Voyages of Coolies from Mauritius to Madras, 1888-91

According to official reports we find in 1888 that 714 coolies had emigrated from Madras to Mauritius and 374 had repatriated to Madras.[53] In 1889 we find 7 ships with 2554 persons had left Madras for Mauritius and 623 emigrants had returned to Madras.[54] The British had poured out licenses to 72 recruiters in Madras for arranging coolies to Mauritius during 1890-91. In all we find 1929 coolies were recruited and the emigrants were sent in ships. In the same year 1891 we find two ships had returned with 306 emigrants to Madras from Mauritius.[55] Those coolies who went for work in the plantations had returned on expiry of the contracts and did not renew for a further period because the working conditions had not been favourable at all.

Coolie labour emigrant like Lotah from Madras who stayed and continued to work in the plantations in Flacq district for long in Mauritius was time and again arrested for deserting the employer for not working as per the contract signed in the sugar plantations. He was arrested on three occasions in 1865, 1881 and 1886 as a vagrant.[56] In February 1865 and in June 1881, on both occasions, he refused to replace his lost old immigrant ticket and police pass. He was sentenced by the Stipendiary Magistrate to serve one week of hard labour at the Vagrant Depot of Grand River. Each time, after serving his sentence, he was sent to the Immigration Depot to obtain a duplicate copy of his Old Immigrant ticket.[57] In 1885, Lotah worked in the Petite Bande and did light work on the Constance Sugar Estate.[58] In 1881 he was photographed and again in 1886 when he was 82 years old again photographed and had to pay one pound sterling for a duplicate copy of his immigrant ticket.[59] The immigrant ticket cost him more than his salary of three months. Finally he requested the Protector of Immigrants for a free return passage to Madras, which was granted. After having lived and worked for more than 55 years, at the age of 85, Lotah left Mauritius and returned to Madras.[60] The living conditions of coolies could be thus be made out since over the decades, the coolies like Lotah had to change the sugar estates where they worked owing to difficulties remaining in the same district of Flacq in Mauritius. Eventually, Lotah returned to Madras in 1889 after having worked and lived in Mauritius for 55 years.

Some Tamils employed in the sugar plantations in Mauritius worked hard and they earned money and saved it for the future. They had acquired properties in the form of liquid assets like cash or jewellery, or immoveable like land and buildings. We find some cases where families sought to make claims against the estate of deceased. They applied to the authorities for the claim of money bequests and inherited sums rightfully due to them. They approached the Immigration Department and through litigation in the colonial courts. We find a case where Alamelu who had arrived as a 1-year old child with her father Veeraa and his wife Velammmal. She had laid claim to the property of her father Veeraa on behalf of herself and her young sister. She did so by petitioning the Protector of Immigrants, requesting that Veeraa's savings, amounting to 800 rupees could be withdrawn from the Savings Bank and invested in landed property. The Immigration Office found out her claim to be legitimate and as legal heir. This was done by tracing Veeraa and his wife through their files and also after finding that they had registered their marriage on arrival in Mauritius.[61]

Further, we find also counter claims to the estates of deceased Tamil immigrants received from blood relatives, seeking to oppose the inheritance rights of spouses or other relatives by marriage. It is found that following the death of Marutha Muthu, his widow Ammani found herself facing a challenge for custody of their children. Their paternal grandfather had petitioned the Supreme Court to this effect, probably as a means of retaining control over his son's assets which included two plots of land. She contacted the Immigration Office who put in a counter-petition on her behalf. A police constable secured the return of the children to their mother and she was eventually made guardian of her husband's property and a notary was appointed to draw up an inventory of Marutha Muthu's estate. She was able to get what was due.[62]

Conclusion

The foregoing pages help us to draw a conclusion that the labour system developed in Mauritius was not certainly static. It had moved from the bounty system and then to contingent system with changes in labour policy. It was also definitely not a new system of slavery. It was an ongoing process of labour recruitment and had complex and dynamic features which involved different human-actors such as the planters in Mauritius, the British colonial officials and the Tamil immigrants. In Mauritius, it was an extremely difficult experience for the British rule because the estate owners did not shed away that easily their despotic habits and failed to pay the wages regularly, did not respect and follow the contractual obligations which they were supposed to do. The planters took a very long period to understand their binding with the coolies and change their mindset to adhere properly to the system of wage labour under a contract in a fair manner. This necessitated for the changes in labour recruitment policy from time to time. As migrants the workers solely and heavily relied only on their wages to subsist which was a very low income. It was 5 rupees per month per head in the beginning, increased to 7 rupees in 1842, and then got raised to 9 rupees in 1865. Thus maintaining a family by the wage was extremely difficult. The difficult living and working conditions in the sugar estates when became hard the coolies deserted estates from the rural and went over to Port Louis the urban centre for earning.

Though in England, sale of coolies was prohibited in 1807 through the efforts of Wilberforce and an act was passed in this regard, Mauritius, the British colony received 835 Indian convicts from Bengal and Bombay in 1815 and they lived in the 'Convicts Barracks' at Grand River North West and Trou Fanfaron and in camps in rural districts. Some convicts were also sent to work on sugar plantations. Some others skilled and so worked as tailors, cooks, cotton spinners, indigo manufacturers, but the importation of convict labour to Mauritius was stopped only in 1838. We find thereafter the recruitment of coolie labourers from Madras to Mauritius. The coolie Tamil emigrants from 1850 to 1890 in total had been 1,19,815 including males, females and children. Indian marriage laws were implemented in Mauritius. These had placed immigrant women under the legal authority of their spouses, effectively marshalling the forces of the state against runaways or adulterers, and criminalizing disobedient wives. The application of law created some confusion and distress among immigrants who attempted to make family arrangements which officials believed contravened colonial legislation. Tamil emigrants who had completed their terms of service in Mauritius could not often return to Madras owing to difficulties in getting return passage when abolished in 1853. Some had escaped or re-emigrated to Reunion the nearby French colony. Some Tamils of course who were outcaste from their native villages in Tamil country consciously thought to remain in Mauritius than returning to Madras. Others who had originally settled in Mauritius had created new families and found some kind of employment saw Mauritius as the colony of their adoption and their real home. In British records we do not find many Tamils had returned to Madras with families too and also sailing on a voyage for a second or third time, moved over to Mauritius if not frequently at least for a time.

Some writers have opined that the commencement of indentured migration coincided with the great era of humanitarian reform. It may be said that whilst philanthropic ideal was in the ascendance, the practice of social welfare was only in its infancy. The introduction and development of institutions like orphanages and asylums in Mauritius aimed to assist the poor and dependent in society, their operation and effects were often punitive. In fact with the flooding of arrival of Tamil coolie labourers in Mauritius they were be treated and mainly used for the British colonial enterprises and the capitalistic development of the colony.

Notes

1. British Library (hereafter BL), Oriental and India Office Collection (hereafter OIOC), P/3/46, pp. 488-93. See also *Calcutta Gazette*, Extraordinary dated 27 July 1789.
2. BL, OIOC, P/241/17, pp. 644, 682.
3. BL, OIOC, F/4/1128/30151.
4. BL, OIOC, F/4/919/25850, p. 134, see the letter of C.M. Lushington to A.D. Campbell dated 1 July 1819.
5. BL, OIOC, F/4/919/25850, p. 174, see the letter of J. Vaughan to the Board of Revenue dated 20 July 1819.
6. BL, OIOC, F/4/1034/28499. Slavery, Kidnapping and Sale of children in Tanjore and Tinnevelly, 1825.
7. BL, OIOC, F/4/1414/55774. Relative to the Kidnapping of Children from the Company's Territory for Sale as Slaves, 1830–33.
8. Vijayalakshmi Teelock, ed., *The Vagrant Depot of Grand River: Its Surroundings and Vagrancy in British Mauritius*: Port Louis, 2004, pp.1-5; C. Barnabas, *From Madras to Mauritius, 1800-1856, Studies in Emigration and Assimilation*, Ph. D. Dissertation, University of Madras, 1991.
9. Mahatma Gandhi Institute (hereafter MGI), Moka, Mauritius, PE Series: Registers 1852-1858.
10. National Archives of Mauritius (hereafter NAM), Coromandel, RA Series: General Correspondence: In-Letters (hereafter RA), 1788, Report of Travelling Inspector, southern districts, 1865, see the reports of Marsh and Marley.
11. NAM, RA Series, 416, see the letter of Finiss to Barry dated 26 October 1829.
12. NAM, RA 417, see the letter of Finiss to Barry dated 27 November 1829; RA 418, Letter of Finiss to Barry dated 17 December 1829; Hugette Ly Tio-Fane Pineo, *Lured Away: The Life History of Cane Workers in Mauritius*, 2nd ed. Moka, 2009, pp. 17-18.
13. NAM, RA 416; RA 417; RA 418.
14. NAM, RA 416, Letter of Finiss to Barry dated 26 October 1829; RA 417, letter of Finiss to Barry dated 27 November 1829; RA 418, Letter of Finiss to Barry dated 17 December 1829.
15. Ibid.
16. MGI, Moka, Mauritius, PE Series: Ship Arrivals and Distribution List of Indentures Labourers, PE 1, Ship Arrivals and Distribution List of Indentured

Labourers for 1826 to 1842; PF Series: Register of Engagements entered into by Immigrants and Others, PF 1, Register of Engagements entered into by Immigrants and Others between 1836 and 1842; NAM, RC Series: Petitions Relative to Indian Immigration, (hereafter RC) 25, Petition of Immigrant Lotah, Ex-Indenture Labourer from Madras, India to Acting Governor Staveley which was drafted on his behalf by the clerk of Argy Sugar Estate upon the instructions of Mr. Hardy in Flacq dated 5 June 1840.

17. NAM, RA 552, Letter of Charles Anderson, Special Magistrate of Port Louis to Mr. Hardy of Argy Sugar Estate dated 30 August 1836; RC 26, Letter of Hardy to Anderson dated 5 September 1836; MGI, IIA/PF 1.
18. NAM, RC 25, see the petition of immigrant Lotah to Acting Governor of Flacq dated 5 June 1840.
19. Tamilnadu State Archives (hereafter TNSA), Chennai, *Accounts and Papers*, vol 25: Correspondence between the Government of India dated 18 September 1838, see also, vol. no. 19, 26 January-22 June 1841, pp. 170-72.
20. MGI, PE Series: Ship Arrivals and Distribution List of Indentures Labourers, PE 1, No. 2415. Vyavry aged 28 from Tamil country a pallar by caste had reached Mauritius in 1838.
21. James Backhouse, *A Narrative of a Visit to the Mauritius and South Africa*, London: Hamilton, Adams, and Co, 1844, pp. 34–7.
22. Ibid., NAM, RC 34, Report of Thomy Hugon on Indian Immigration to Governor Sir William Nicolay dated 15 July 1839.
23. *Le Mauricien*, 15 February 1839; Satyendra Peerthum, Reconsidering Crime in Port Louis: African apprentices and Indian Labourers' in A. Boraine, et al. eds., *The Report of the Truth and Justice Commission: Volume 4: History, Economy, Society and Memory: Part VIII: Indentured Immigration*. Port Louis, 2011, p. 198.
24. Hugh Tinker, *A New System of Slavery: The Export of Indian Labour Overseas, 1830-1920*, 1974, pp. 54-6.
25. Marina Carter, *Servants, Sirdars and Settlers: Indians in Mauritius, 1834-1874*, New Delhi, OUP, 1995, see chapter two.
26. BL, OIOC, *Madras Public Proceedings* (herefater MPP), 247/63, see the letter of Finniss to the Colonial Secretary dated 18 June 1841.
27. NAM, RA Series, See the Report Diary of Grierson, p. 9.
28. NAM, RA Series, See the deposition of Vaithilinga Nayakkar taken by the magistrate of Thanjavur on 13 June and 25 June 1857.
29. BL, *Parlimentary Papers 1846*, XXVIII (691-I), see the enclosures of Neave Report.
30. BL, OIOC, MPP, 248/8, see the letter of Emigration Agent to the Secretary of the Government of Madras dated 21 September 1843.
31. NAM, PA Series, 57, see the letter of the Emigration Agent to the Secretary of the Government of Madras dated 24 February 1843.
32. NAM, RA Series, 1081, see the letter of the Emigration Agent of Madras to the Colonial Secretary dated 2 September 1850; see also the contract between Henry Wood Gabb, the Emigration Agent and the contractor P.A. Pillay in March 1850.

33. NAM, RC Series, Report 244.
34. NAM, RA Series, see the travelling reports on the tour of the northern districts between August 1865 and January 1866.
35. BL, *British Parliamentary Papers* (hereafter BPP), Annual Series, 1844, vol. 35, p. 530, see the letter of Tennent to Hope dated 21 March 1843.
36. David Northrup, *Indentured Labor in the Age of Imperialism, 1834-1922*, Cambridge, 1995, pp. 74-5.
37. BL, OIOC, MPP, 248/8, Letter of Emigration Agent to Secretary to Government, Madras, dated 21 September 1843.
38. Vijayalakshmi Teelock, *Mauritius Indentured Labour and Society, 1835-1935*, Moka, 2001, pp. 964-6.
39. V. Lalitha, 'Emigration of British Subjects from French Ports in India to French Colonies-Proposal to Legalise – Papers Relating to Down to 1858', *Revue Historique de Pondichery*, no. XIII, 1976 - 80, pp. 162-168, see pp. 162-3.
40. *A Collection of the Laws of Mauritius and its Dependencies, 2 February 1852 to 31 December 1853*, 1867, vol. VI, p. 123.
41. NAM, PB Series: Letters of the Protector of Immigrants to other Government Departments (hereafter PB) 5, Protector's Report, 13 November 1855; PA Series: Letters received by the Protector of Immigrants from other Government Departments (hereafter PA) 14, letter of M. Perot to M. Aubin dated 10 October 1872; PA 12, District Magistrate of Grand Port, Report no. 206 of 1871.
42. V. Lalitha, Emigration of British Subjects, p. 166.
43. BPP, Annual series, XLVII (314), Report by J. Geoghegan on Coolie Emigration from India, 1874, pp. 67-68.
44. *A Collection of the Laws of Mauritius and its Dependencies,* 1868, vol. VII, p. 665, see the ordiance no. 30 of 1858.
45. *Report on the Moral and Material Progress and Conditions of India, 1860-61*, p. 292.
46. BPP, Cmnd. 1115 -1, Appendix B to Royal Commissioners' Report no 38; see also, Report of Enquiry into the case of Calleemoottoo, see the letter of Jenner to Protector dated 25 August 1872.
47. Hugh Tinker, A New System of Slavery, p. 102.
48. J.K. Chapman, *The Career of Arthur Hamilton Gordon*, Toronto, 1964, pp. 118-20, 128-9.
49. NAM, PL 79, Petition of Nagen and Camatchee dated 8 September 1868; PA 14 Letter of Inspector of Government Reformatory to Beyts dated 26 January 1872.
50. BPP, Annual series, XLVII (314), Report by J. Geoghegan on Coolie Emigration from India, 1874, p. 66.
51. NAM, PA 68, Poor Law Commissioner to Protector of Immigrants, Protector's note dated 28 April 1885; Immigration Office Note dated 29 April 1885.
52. NAM, PA 204, Immigration Department Minutes, dated 14 September 1899.
53. *Report on the Moral and Material Progress and Conditions of India, 1887 -88*, p. 155.

54. *Report on the Moral and Material Progress and Conditions of India, 1888-89*, p. 172.
55. *Report on the Moral and Material Progress and Conditions of India, 1889-90*, p. 194.
56. MGI, PO Series: Vagrancy, Desertion and Illegal Absence Registers (hereafter PO), PO 10, vol. B, Warrants issued against Indian Immigrants for Vagrancy for the period between 1855 and 1878; PH Series: Vagrant Register with Vagrant Pictures (hereafter PH), 2, Vagrant Register for the period between 1870 to 1889; PI Series: Register of Passes issued to Immigrants reported by the Police to have lost their tickets (hereafter PI), 4, Register of Passes issued to Immigrants reported by the Police and to have lost their Tickets between1882 and 1906.
57. NAM, RA 1804, Letter of the Stipendiary Magistrate of Flacq to the Protector of Immigrants dated 21 February 1865; MNA, PA 48, Letter of the Stipendiary Magistrate of Flacq to the Protector of Immigrants dated 4 June 1881; MGI, PO Series: Vagrancy, Desertion and Illegal Absence Registers, (hereafter PO), PO 10, vol. B; PI 4.
58. MGI, PF Series: Register of Engagements entered into by Immigrants and Others, (hereafter PF), PF 44, 1885.
59. MGI, Immigrant No. 3158, Photograph of Lotah at the Immigration Depot, MGI, PG Series: Immigrant Photo Registers, (hereafter PG), PG 32, Immigrant Photo Register for 1886; PE Series: Ship Arrivals and Distribution List of Indentures Labourers, see, PE 1; PG 32; see also PH 2; PI 4.
60. NAM, PA 111, Petition of Immigrant Lotah submitted on his behalf by the clerk of Constance Sugar Estate to the Protector of Immigrants on 22 June 1889; MGI, PJ Series: List of Returning Immigrants, (hereafter PJ), /PJ 41, Register of Indenture Ship Departures for 1880 to 1910.
61. NAM, PA 60, Letter of Allamalloo to Protector of Immigrants dated 8 March 1884; Immigration Office note dated 12 March 1884.
62. NAM, PA 206, Letter of Ameenee to Protector of Immigrants dated 19 October 1899.

Chapter - 5

Migration of Wage Labour Tamils to Ceylon and the Social Life of the Migrants in the Coffee Plantations under the British, 1828-83

With the conquest of Kandy the inland kingdom in Ceylon in 1815 the British politically aimed to unify the island. It was felt necessary at that time to plan and arrange for the migration of Tamils to populate the island and develop the economy. Immediate steps were taken and the British collector of Thanjavur in Tamil country in 1815 was asked by the Government of Madras to make use of all the means in his power to drive coolies and cattle to Ceylon. The collector politely informed that the Government of Ceylon would have to send agents to recruit coolies and should think of offering special inducements to the labourers because they were reluctant to migrate away from their homeland.[1] As a result, the Government of Ceylon established private concerns for the recruitment of cheap labour force for their coffee plantations. It was also considered by them as more efficient than the official agencies. In 1818 the Assistant Commissioner in Ceylon wrote to the collector of Thanjavur that the Government had satisfactorily entered into direct contract with *maistries* (chiefs) who would act as labour contractors agreeing to find around 600 labourers. This happened when the Ceylon Government began with the construction of a road from the coastal capital of Colombo to Kandy, which primarily aimed at bringing the Kandyans under closer control of the colonial power after the Kandyan's rebellion in 1818.

Tamil labour migration to Ceylon did not pick up speed as desired by the British because there was reluctance on the part of the workers. Ten years later (1828) Barnes, the Governor of Ceylon made steps to recruit free labour and he could bring 150 Tamil coolies for the coffee plantation. Within a year all these men deserted. These workers, when they found other planters offered more money, abandoned their contracts.[2] Thus, we notice that migration between Tamil country and Ceylon had not been brisk and active. Migrant workers were not subjected to government control. They were also not bound by indenture. Lax of the government control and the pronounced economic interest of the hosts led to frequent abuses of the labour system. The availability of a cheap and steady workforce soon became much more important than of the welfare of the workers.

It is known from records that Sinhalese labourers were recruited and working in the plantations under a *kangaani* (overseer/headman/foreman in Tamil) in 1838. Frederick Lewis the planter had described the workforce employed on his estate of Sinhalese origin.[3] The illegal export of coolies in 1841 was mainly carried on by the French through the port of Pondicherry. An investigation by the British Collector of South Arcot district had disclosed the traffic of people to Ceylon. T. W. Baynes, a judge, had written on behalf of his brother, a coffee planter near Colombo to Charles Dickens, a trader in Cuddalore on 10 February 1841 that the labour in Ceylon was somewhat scarce and high in price. Hence his brother had been very anxious to have some coolie labourers from the Tamil coast. He stated that the Singalese coolies were very idle and they received nine rupees per month. He also said that he would be happy if Dickens could be successful in arranging coolies and send around 31 labourers to Colombo in a local craft by paying a sum of twelve *annas* towards the cost of passage.[4]

Landlessness and a willingness to work for wages by Tamil immigrants to Ceylon had begun widely only after 1839. The development of coffee plantations in Ceylon had enhanced the sustained demand for Tamil labour. Thus the systematic recruitment to Ceylon had started when 2432 males, 188 females and 99 children came as indentured labourers to a total of 2719 were brought in ships in 1839. The number had been increasing till 1842 when 9025 males, 279 females and 166 children amounting to a total of 9470 reached Ceylon. Thus migrants had increased to around four folds within four years.

Tamil Labour Immigration to Ceylon, 1839-42

Year	*Males*	*Females*	*Children*	*Total*
1839	2432	188	99	2719
1840	3326	307	181	3814
1841	4523	363	164	5050
1842	9025	279	166	9470
Total	**19306**	**1137**	**610**	**21053**

Source: National Archives of the United Kingdom, Kew, Ceylon Blue Books, 1839-1842, Colonial Office Records, 54/250; Governor's Despatch Miscellaneous no.6 of 21 April 1847 to the Secretary of State for Colonies, p. 207.

The cultivation of coffee in Ceylon had spread on the island and the system was pure export of monoculture, and relied exclusively on imported wage labour from Tamil country. Thus, it is surprising that annual labour immigration—a process was vital to the efficient functioning of the plantation economy and it received practically no government attention in the beginning.

Departure of Labourers from Ceylon to Tamil Coast, 1839-42

Year	*Males*	*Females*	*Children*	*Total*
1839	1956	161	85	2202
1840	3464	256	3	3723
1841	4243	279	120	4642
1842	10691	345	228	11264
Total	**20354**	**1041**	**436**	**21831**

Source: National Archives of the United Kingdom, Kew, Ceylon Blue Books, 1839-1842, Colonial Office Records, 54/250; Governor's Despatch Miscellaneous no.6 of 21 April 1847 to the Secretary of State for Colonies, p. 207.

Tamil labourers also left the island on expiry of the contract period of one year. The departure was very regular and annual. It is surprising to note that 778 more labourers who went prior to 1839 had preferred to return to homeland within four years. We have no clue as to the number of deaths occurred. It must be borne in mind that returning to Tamil country was simple and easy for the motherland was located close to the island of Ceylon.

According to records an ordinance was passed in 1841. The objective of this the Service Contracts Ordinance No. 5 of 1841 was set out as the better regulation of servants, labourers and journeymen artificers, under contracts for hire and service. It applied to any menial or domestic servant or labourer in the service of Government, or of any person or persons. A written contract signed by both parties could be made valid for a period of one year and was terminable by one month's notice. The contract was enforced through the penal provision in Section 7 of the Ordinance.[5] The rigorous contracts binding the labourers in the system thus had several functional equivalents in free labour migration. The ordinance had a clause which indicated the planters in Ceylon to take criminal action against the labourers who broke contract.

It is observed by 1844 the labour recruitment in Tamil country had become highly functional and common. The Planters' Association in Ceylon reported that the owner of Black Forest Estate had sent a recruiter to Tamil coast in 1844 who later returned with 14 workers.[6] Thus the labour recruitment system had developed with a *kangaani*. Under this, a labourer already in employment at the plantation in Ceylon was sent by his employer to recruit labourers from his village or other places in Tamil country. This was adopted preferably because of the relatively lower cost involved in sending a *kangaani* to recruit labour than the escalating price to be paid to the recruiting agencies. *Kangaani* was felt as a powerful intermediary and a reliable man and he received 'head money' from each recruited worker for every day worked, which was forfeited if the worker absconded. The labour immigrants thereafter came in boats and ships to Ceylon in groups by 1847. The *kangaani* conducted journey by overland in Tamil country, brought them in sailing vessels, negotiated their engagements later superintended their labour, in return for which he also received from each of his subordinates a trifling part of their pay.[7]

It must be mentioned that migrants were organized by *kangaani*, who was responsible for them at every stage of their journey to the plantations. He was the recruiting-officer in Tamil country, who visited the villages of his native region to persuade persons whose social background was normally agricultural labourers and indebted peasants to accompany him to work on the coffee plantations for varying lengths of time from one year to three years.[8] The *kangaanis* travelled with the groups of Tamils varying from 25 to 100 coolies, all the way from the place of recruitment to Ceylon, advancing them the money required on their journey to reach the plantations. Thereafter the *kangaani* continued to act as supervisor and was responsible to the plantation owners and managers for the workers he had brought who were usually also indebted to him for the cash advances given.[9] The labour recruitment system was thus simple and the role of the *kangaanis* was very important because of the social and financial powers they exercised within the limited geography of the plantations. The advantages of the system were naturally distributed. The migrants were taken care of from beginning to end without having to risk anything in the process of transplantation except their freedom and health. The *kangaani* and the planter shared the profits from a labour force that could be recruited in the most flexible manner. Thus the contact and contract between labour and capital had been well established.

Regarding the voyage, according to sources it is gleaned that persons recruited generally walked from village to the port of Tuticorin and then travelled by sea to reach Colombo. Boats from Rameswaram and to Thalaimannar also sailed carrying labourers and after four or five hours of journey stopped at Adam's Bridge, and then sailed from Thalaimannar to Arippu on west coast of Ceylon to reach the coffee plantations.[10] It has been mentioned in 1846 and 1847 that those who sailed away from Tuticorin were usually from Tirunelveli and Madurai districts. The planters in Ceylon had found it far more expensive than the route of Rameswaram.[11] The labour migration had drastically increased between 1843 and 1849 when compared to the previous period.

Tamil Labour Immigration to Ceylon, 1843-9

Year	*Males*	*Females*	*Children*	*Total*
1843	35195	957	448	36600
1844	74840	957	724	76521
1845	72526	698	177	73401
1846	41862	330	125	42317
1847	44085	1638	417	46140
1848	29936	1685	551	32172
1849	22171	1430	268	23869
Total	**320615**	**7695**	**2710**	**331020**

Source: National Archives of the United Kingdom, Kew, Ceylon Blue Books, 1843-1849, Colonial Office Records, 54/227, 54/235, 54/250; Governor's Despatch Miscellaneous no.6 of 21 April 1847 to the Secretary of State for Colonies, p. 207.

On arrival the immigrant workers were asked to stay in the large sheds which were halls prepared for them to reside. The workers preferred smaller rooms because they would be warmer and cozy. This had been mentioned by the planters in 1845.[12] The coffee plantation owners failed to pay the wages of the Tamil workers in 1846. Hence the labourers unpaid for months had stopped doing work. Mr. Harrington one of the estate owners had whipped a man to death which had been reported.[13]

Muthusamy a Tamil labourer immigrant recruited to work in Ceylon in 1847 was not used to the new climate. He needed a *kambali* (woolen blanket) because he had to work in the estate which was 2000 feet above the sea level. The blanket was supplied but the cost was debited against him.[14]

Owing to unhygienic conditions in the coffee estates with the spread of disease the labourers who became sick around 164 were admitted at the hospitals at Gampola, Kuregalle, Puttalam and Matale. The death of Tamil labourers in 1847 had accounted for 85 persons a rate of 51.82%.[15] However, we find around 19824 workers had annually returned from Ceylon to Tamil coast during the seven years between 1843 and 1849.

Departure of Labourers from Ceylon to Tamil Coast, 1843-9

Year	*Males*	*Females*	*Children*	*Total*
1843	18977	694	482	20153
1844	38337	825	535	39697
1845	24623	145	36	24804
1846	13833	48	25	13906
1847	5897	74	33	6004
1848	22680	557	152	23389
1849	10397	335	83	10815
Total	**134744**	**2678**	**1346**	**138768**

Source: National Archives of the United Kingdom, Kew, Ceylon Blue Books, 1843-1849, Colonial Office Records, 54/227, 54/235, 54/250; Governor's Despatch Miscellaneous no.6 of 21 April 1847 to the Secretary of State for Colonies, p. 207.

A schooner of 29 tons from Tuticorin carried 201 persons in a single trip in 1853 and reached Colombo. Another sailing vessel of 80 tons had sailed away with 400 people on board and reached Ceylon.[16] The British Government officials were attentive to the needs of the immigrants and they inspected and also looked after it on the route from the port in Tamil country to the estate in Ceylon.[17] However, the mortality could not but have decreased. Sheds were made available on the land route but the immigrants were not allowed to use them unless it was raining. The supply of water was also scarce and bad at every station on the route till they reached the estate. Kankasabhai a Tamil *kangaani* to a planter in an estate in Matale East had reported this news vide his letter dated 30 May 1857.[18] The outbreak of the sepoy mutiny in India in 1857 seems to have had some impact for we find increasing number of immigrants sailing in boats from Tamil Country to Ceylon in 1857 and 1858.

Tamil Labour Immigration to Ceylon, 1850-61

Year	*Males*	*Females*	*Children*	*Total*
1850	37155	1818	449	39422
1851	28224	1003	273	29500
1852	50843	2226	770	53839
1853	36583	2042	653	39278
1854	54014	9006	4301	67321
1855	55979	5018	1270	62267
1856	59263	6342	2399	68004
1857	60048	6974	2298	69320
1858	75172	16172	4718	96062
1859	32377	5797	1911	40085
1860	41906	8946	2093	52945
1861	43147	8175	2110	53432
Total	**574711**	**73519**	**23245**	**671475**

Source: National Archives of the United Kingdom, Kew, Ceylon Blue Books, 1850-1861; Ferguson's Ceylon Directory, 1866-68, p. 183; R. Jayaraman, 'Indian Emigration to Ceylon: Some Aspects of the Historical and Social Background of the Emigrants', Indian Economic and Social History Review, vol. 4, no. 4, December, 1967, pp 319-59, see pp. 322, 324.

Return of the immigrant labourers had continued from Ceylon to Tamil country. On expiry of the contracts the workers decided to leave for the homeland. It is mentioned that an immigrant who was returning in 1857 with his savings from Ceylon to Tamil country was subjected to exploitation.[19]

Departure of Labourers from Ceylon to Tamil Coast, 1850-61

Year	*Males*	*Females*	*Children*	*Total*
1850	20758	548	303	21609
1851	16775	419	191	1738
1852	22664	780	284	23728
1853	27129	981	378	28488
1854	21640	1422	479	23541
1855	23130	573	313	24016
1856	32148	1502	659	34309
1857	36887	2278	772	39937
1858	45747	3277	1416	50440
1859	43900	3722	1196	48818
1860	21279	1874	721	23874
1861	32636	3487	1079	37202
Total	**344693**	**20863**	**7791**	**373347**

Source: National Archives of the United Kingdom, Kew, Ceylon Blue Books, 1850-1861; Ferguson's Ceylon Directory, 1866-68, p. 183; R. Jayaraman, 'Indian Emigration to Ceylon: Some Aspects of the Historical and Social Background of the Emigrants', Indian Economic and Social History Review, vol. 4, no. 4, December, 1967, pp 319-59, see pp. 322, 324.

As the labour migration from Tamil Country to Ceylon had been developing the British Crown introduced a system of official control in 1862. Therefore the British Raj had set up one camp for the labour migrants to assemble at Thatapaarai for those leaving the port of Tuticorin and another camp at Mandapam was erected for those leaving from Rameswaram.[20] Recruitment of Labourers had developed all over the districts in Tamil country. The number of migrants too swelled up very high annually.

Tamil Labour Immigration to Ceylon, 1862-70

Year	*Males*	*Females*	*Children*	*Total*
1862	51859	12503	4534	68896
1863	53828	11858	5032	70718
1864	63087	14214	4499	81800
1865	66007	16831	6759	89597
1866	58488	23723	6117	88328
1867	31688	8836	2255	42779
1868	41499	11540	2682	55721
1869	43998	11150	2523	57671
1870	51,644	10835	2735	65214
Total	**462098**	**121490**	**37136**	**620724**

Source: National Archives of the United Kingdom, Kew, Ceylon Blue Books, 1862-1870; Ferguson's Ceylon Directory, 1866-68, p. 183; R. Jayaraman, 'Indian Emigration to Ceylon: Some Aspects of the Historical and Social Background of the Emigrants', Indian Economic and Social History Review, vol. 4, no. 4, December, 1967, pp 319-59, see p. 325.

It is found in records that government ferries and native boats had transported separately Tamil labourers to Ceylon. In 1863 government ferries transported 69347 labourers while the native boats had carried 1371 amounting to a total of 70718 labourers. Similarly, in 1864 government ferries transported 81,800 labourers while native boats had carried 2200 amounting to a total of 84,000 labourers. British officials like O'Brien was of the opinion that there should be a regular service by the steamship company which had proposed to run ships in 1864 between Madras and Nagapattinam to Colombo with the government subsidy.[21]

Departure of Labourers from Ceylon to Tamil Coast, 1862-70

Year	*Males*	*Females*	*Children*	*Total*
1862	51859	12503	4534	68896
1863	53828	11858	5032	70718
1864	63087	14214	4499	81800

(*Contd...*)

1865	66007	16831	6759	89597
1866	58488	23723	6117	88328
1867	31688	8836	2255	42779
1868	41499	11540	2682	55721
1869	43998	11150	2523	57671
1870	51,644	10835	2735	65214
Total	462098	121490	37136	620724

Source: C.D. Maclean, Manual of the Madras Presidency, The Government Press, Madras, 1885, pp. 502-3. National Archives of the United Kingdom, Kew, Ceylon Blue Books, 1862-1870; Ferguson's Ceylon Directory, 1866-68, p. 183; R. Jayaraman, 'Indian Emigration to Ceylon: Some Aspects of the Historical and Social Background of the Emigrants', Indian Economic and Social History Review, vol. 4, no. 4, December, 1967, pp 319-59, see p. 325.

It is gleaned from the statistics that around 126064 labourers stayed in Ceylon without returning to Tamil country during 1862 and 1870. The British Crown desired to introduce new legal provisions in the then existed of Ordinance 5 of 1841. Therefore refined provisions had been included in 1865 and the Ordinance 11 of 1865 came into force.[22] In short, the Master and Servant Laws regulated the duties of a servant/plantation labourer and identified three actions of such labourers leading to criminal prosecution. It included the neglect of duty (e.g. late attendance, refusal to work etc.,) a wide array of misconduct in service (e.g. drunkenness, disobedience, etc.,) and the quitting of service without one month's prior notice.[23] A labourer who was found guilty of one of these charges was liable to a fine of up to 5 pounds or up to three months imprisonment. The only offence on the part of the employer recognized by the Master and Servant Laws was the refusal to pay wages.

The Ordinance 11 of 1865 obliged the employer to provide his labourers with lodging, food and medical care during periods of sickness, and refusal to pay wages. The Master and Servant Laws had recognized the free nature of plantation labour. All labour relations particularly the terminations of the contracts were regulated on the basis of verbal one-month notice. There existed all possibility to enter into longer written contracts. In theory, the labourer could leave an estate at one month's notice. In reality, a number of customs and practices of plantation recruitment and life kept the bulk of the immigrant labour force from enforcing their rights as laid down in the legislation. The rigid hierarchy of the *kangaani* system and an evolving network of debt bondage served as functional equivalents and secured the availability of a cheap and steady labour force. In the rising demand for labour, the recruitments were made and the migration had been on the increasing side from 1867 to 1883.

Tamil Labour Migration to Ceylon, 1871-83

Year	*Number of Workers*
1871	89529
1872	75456
1873	88418
1874	117227
1875	87509
1876	184919
1877	152073
1878	99146
1879	63344
1880	43292
1881	46594
1882	45055
1883	35292
Total	**1127854**

Source: C.D. Maclean, Manual of the Madras Presidency, The Government Press, Madras, 1885, pp. 502-3.

According to sources labour migrants on a large scale took place during the famine years of 1876 and 1878.[24] Nicholson the acting collector of Madurai in 1877 reported to the Board of Revenue in Madras that several hamlets and villages in his district were almost deserted. The people were digging for the root of Indian turnip to eat in the land but yet could not find. They starved very much and had absolutely nothing to eat. People from Madurai area migrated to Tirunelveli during the famine period. The collector of Madurai in his report to the Board of Revenue recorded that the streams of the people were pouring into Ceylon from Rameswaram too. One third of the males had migrated from southwest Ramanathapuram. One member of each family had migrated to Ceylon in some cases, and in other cases the houses were shut up and all had gone.[25] The route to coffee plantations through Puttalam and Anurudhapura was direct and cheaper and so the labourers on arrival were taken to the coffee plantations. The working hours in the estate were from 6 am to 10 am and again from 12 noon to 5.30 pm. The labourers worked six days in a week. They were paid 15 shillings per month.

Though the enormous influx of labour immigrants from Tamil country had been recorded in British sources, a close look at the statistics reveal that majority of the labour migrants hailed from the district of Tirunelveli from 1865 to 1874.[26] A ratio of one fifth of total labour recruited and migrated was from Tirunelveli district to Ceylon during the ten years.

Labour migration from Tirunelveli District to Ceylon, 1865-74

Year	*Workers*
1865	21256
1866	16941
1867	9911
1868	9501
1869	11793
1870	12905
1871	14627
1872	16486
1873	17876
1874	23887
Total	**155183**

Source: C.D. Maclean, Manual of the Madras Presidency, The Government Press, Madras, 1885, pp. 502-3.

It has been reported by Roger in Ceylon in 1867 that he did not doubt that the coolies were better off in the island than in India. In his opinion he justified that if this was not so the coolies would not have come to Ceylon.[27] It is reported that debts of 2 to 5 pounds by the coolies to the estate by means was uncommon and this debt was a mere trifle.[28] Abraham Joseph one of the Tamil *kangaanis* mentioned in 1869 that happiness and privileges the coolies enjoyed on the estates were manifold.[29] He stated that there was no way for a *kangaani* to cheat his coolies because the fact is that the labourers would pay off their debts and contract directly with the planters.[30]

A. Joseph published a book in 1869 titled '*Kopi Krishi Kummi*' wherein we find that he had dedicated the work to the coffee estate owners in Ceylon. It states that the Tamil workers sang folk songs during their time of duty in the coffee estate and at other times of rest and leisure. These *kummi* songs in Tamil have been collected and compiled by him and this piece of work serves as an alternate to the objectionable songs and so he had desired to present them in a different tone.[31] A. Joseph had published another book titled 'The Planters' Colloquial Tamil Guide' in 1872. This book was written to facilitate learning of Tamil by the British planters in Ceylon so as to mange the Tamil labourers. It is my opinion that the everyday life of the Tamil labourers in the coffee estate had been mildly expressed by A. Joseph and the negative aspects had been not well described. He seems to have supported the cause of the planters for he was employed as a *kangaani* and so had solely aimed to depict the management of the coffee estate by the planters.[32] Alexander Brown published in 1872 the Coffee Planters Manual wherein he had condemned the weakness of some planters who drank often too excess and extravagance.[33]

It is found mention in 1870 that a room of 12 feet square with a small verandah should accommodate ten immigrants. This suggestion was made by Sabonadiere one of the coffee planters of Ceylon.[34] Gregory who visited Ceylon in 1872 mentioned that he had seen a great deal of the island and he was fully convinced that there was not a labouring population in any part of the world so well off. Labour was of such important in Ceylon that a planter dare not ill treat his coolies for fear of his plantation getting a bad name.[35]

The coffee leaf disease spread had begun to wipe out Ceylon's coffee plantations in the late 1870s. It is found in records of 1874 that planters in Ceylon had continued to employ private agencies to recruit coolies in Tamil country. Those coolies recruited and sent to Ceylon were found useless and they fled when being made to work hard. In this case the labourers did not have a *kangaani* to keep them in hand.[36] Even during the year 1880 it is reported that 21374 labourers had migrated from the district of Tirunelveli to Ceylon. When we compare the figure of 43292 migrants from Tamil country to Ceylon in 1880 we find still 50% of the migrants were from Tirunelveli district. The Government of Ceylon became directly involved in immigrant labour policy only in the year 1880 through the enactment of the Medical Wants Ordinance. For the first time, it took over direct responsibility for the medical treatment of the immigrant labourers thus paying tribute to the enormously high death rate among plantation workers. Thus labour migration from Tamil Country to Ceylon had been facilitated largely through less control and power exercised by the authorities in British India and also not very rigid and strict systems of labour policy adopted in Ceylon.

Conclusion

The geographical proximity and cultural closeness had been the ideal conditions for the massive transfer of labour from Tamil country to Ceylon. The first Tamil labourers arrived in 1828 and their numbers increased in the course of the following decades. Labourers bound by a contract for one year in the beginning migrated and returned but it was impossible for them to withdraw before the expiry of contract. The immigrants were later subject to a quasi-military regimentation and the labour recruitment was replaced by the *kangaani* system. This system used community ties as the means of recruitment and the contractors used the market. The period of the contract was enhanced to three years in many cases. Tamil labour had been secured in Ceylon by contractors since 1837, and was uncontrolled by the Government of India. In 1847 the Ceylon government proposed an ordinance for the protection of Indian coolies, which led to Act XIII of that year. In 1861 a further ordinance relating to contracts for the hire and service of labourers in the country was proposed. There was some dissent over the ordinance at first, but in 1862 the Indian government stated that it was satisfied with Ceylon's system for protecting Indian labourers. Therefore migration had been conducted very smoothly.

The coffee cultivation in Ceylon that began in 1830 was the major modern enterprise in Ceylon set by the British capital. Between 1835 and 1837 we find 4000 to 5000 acres of forest land had been cleared and planted with coffee around Kandy. During the 1860s, the offer of extremely lucrative land grants by the colonial government stimulated a speculative boom in coffee cultivation. The area devoted to coffee expanded to 31,843 hectares within a span of 5 to 6 years. In 1841 alone 14,973 hectares had been planted. Most of the entrepreneurs were British partnership owners who were based in Ceylon and Great Britain mainly employees or ex-employees of the English East India Company. The boom busted in 1847 with the fall of coffee prices. By the next decade the coffee industry was on the road to recovery and the area expanded to 71,225 hectares by 1869. Coffee production went into a decline afterwards due to a fungus outbreak, shrinking from 101,981 hectares in 1880 to 39,659 hectares in 1886.

We find that labour migration from Tamil country to Ceylon responded to crop failures, bad seasons, droughts, famines or other environmental calamities. The number of landless agricultural labourers had increased over the periods and it created a demand for ready cash for migration from Tamil country to Ceylon. Migration between Tamil country and Ceylon was free of government control, support or regulation. Instead, certain functional equivalents—such as the *kangaani* system—organized immigration and coordinated supply and demand. Only very late in the nineteenth century, when the *kangaani* system had revealed a number of dramatic organizational weaknesses, the Ceylon Government started to get directly involved in labour and immigration policy. During the 1880s, the coffee plantations in Ceylon were superseded by plantations of a new crop—tea. Labour market in Ceylon was never in excess of the demand. The immigrant started his estate life in debt to the *kangaani* or the planter. *Kangaani* the agent of the planter was pronounced with an advance to secure labour but this advance was debited against Muthusamy and the others he brought over as found in records. Thus *kangaani* was the banker of the labourers and their spokesman.

In the case of non-indentured immigration to Ceylon, where the notion of free immigration was floated by the contemporary official reports and planters, the *kangaani* operated through a system of debt and advances, which tied labour to particular employers. The mediating agency of *kangaanis*, while outside the purview of Governments, did not emerge independently of the network of employers. One significant feature was the immobilization of the mobilized labour force within the plantation complexes both under indenture and *kangaani* systems. The nature of work process adopted and the frenetic pace of expansion of coffee plantations in Ceylon during the nineteenth century did not create residential compulsion for the labour force. The flow to Ceylon in large part was migration rather than emigration. The native Singalese never disliked the Tamil new comers. In fact the Tamils were welcomed by the British planters.

Notes

1. Roland Wenzlhuemer, 'Indian Labour Immigration and British Labour Policy in Nineteenth-Century Ceylon', *Modern Asian Studies*, vol. 41, no. 3, 2007, pp. 575–602.
2. Ibid. See also, M. Roberts, 'Indian Estate Labour in Ceylon During the Coffee Period, 1830–1880, Part 1', *Indian Economic and Social History Review*, vol. 3, no. 1, 1966, pp. 1–52.
3. F. Lewis, *Sixty-Four Years in Ceylon: Reminiscences of Life and Adventure*, Colombo, 1926, pp. 191–92.
4. Hugh Tinker, *A New System of Slavery: The Export of Indian Labour Overseas, 1830-1920*, London, 1974, p. 70.
5. E. Valentine Daniel, 'Violent Measures in the Discursive Practices of Sri Lanka's Estate Tamils', *Comparative Studies in Society and History*, vol. 35, no.3, July 1993, pp 568-600, see p. 570.
6. The National Archives of the United Kingdom (hereafter NAUK), Kew, Colonial Office Records (hereafter CO), 56/2, Ceylon Acts 1841–1843.
7. P. Peebles, *The Plantation Tamils of Ceylon: New Historical Perspectives on Migration*, London, 2001, p. 27.
8. NAUK, CO, 54/235, See the letter of Tennent to Grey dated 21 April 1847; CO, 54/243, see the letter of Torrington to Grey dated 25 February 1847.
9. NAUK, Emerson Tennent the Governor of Ceylon's Despatch Miscelleaneous no. 6 of 21 April 1847 to the Secretary of State for Colonies, p. 207
10. Ibid, R. Jayaraman, 'Indian Emigration to Ceylon: Some Aspects of the Historical and Social Background of the Emigrants', *Indian Economic and Social History Review*, vol. 4, no. 4, December, 1967, pp 319-59.

11. NAUK, CO, 54/299, See the letter of Anderson dated 20 May 1853.
12. NAUK, CO 54/238, See the Confidential letter of Torrington to Grey dated 16 August 1847.
13. Sampson Brown, *Life in the Jungle*, Colombo, 1845, see letter 3.
14. NAUK, CO, 54/227, See the letter of Campbell to Grey dated 11 November 1846.
15. NAUK, CO, 54/235 Tennent to Earl Grey, 21 March 1847.
16. NAUK, CO, 54/235, See the letter of Tennent to Grey dated 21 April 1847.
17. NAUK, CO, 54/299, See the letter of Anderson dated 20 May 1853.
18. National Archives of Sri Lanka (hereafter NASL), Colombo, Lot 41/163, No. 47 of 24 April 1856 and No. 128 of 1 July 1856.
19. Colombo Observer, dated 15 June 1857, Letter of P. Canacaseppa reporting on the North Road dated 30 May 1857.
20. Colombo Observer, 15 June 1857, letter of P. Canacaseppa dated 30 May 1857.
21. Report on Accounts and Paper: House of Commons for Colonies: Immigration vol. XVI, p. 109; See also Report from Commissioners: Emigration Commission, Factories, Mines and Public Health, vol. XXII, 1862, pp. 43-47.
22. NAUK, CO,54/391.
23. NAUK, CO, 56/9, Ceylon Acts 1864–1869; See also, Ceylon Acts, CO 56/2; CO 56/12; M. Roberts, 'The Master–Servant Laws of 1841 and the 1860s and Immigrant Labour in Ceylon', *Ceylon Journal of Historical and Social Studies*, vol. 8, nos. 1-2, 1965, pp. 24-37.
24. R. Weerakoon, *The Evolution of Labour Law in Sri Lanka: Tea Plantation to Free Trade Zone*, Colombo, 1986, pp. 112–13.
25. M. Roberts, 'Indian Estate Labour in Ceylon during the Coffee Period, 1830–1880, Part 2', *Indian Economic and Social History Review*, vol. 3, no. 2, 1966, 101-36, see, pp. 103–04.
26. Ambirajan 'Malthusian Population Theory and Indian Famine Policy in the Nineteenth Century', *Population Studies*, vol. 30, March 1976, pp. 6-7.
27. NAUK, CO, 54/425, Robinson to Earl of Carnaron, No. 57, 6 March 1867, see the minute by Roger dated 22 May 1867.
28. A. M. Ferguson, *The Ceylon Districts for 1866-68*, Colombo, 1868, p. 108.
29. Ceylon Observer, 12 March 1869, A. Joseph, A Tamil's account of the coffee districts of Ceylon.
30. Ceylon Observer, 13 March 1869, A. Joseph, A Tamil's account of the coffee districts of Ceylon.
31. Abraham Joseph, *Kopikrishi Kummi*, Colombo, 1869.
32. Abraham Joseph, *The Planters' Colloquial Tamil Guide and Roman Characters Or the Art of Speaking, Reading and Writing Tamil without a Teacher,* Colombo, 1872. The printed book has 223 pages.
33. Alexander Brown, *The Coffee Planter's Manual*, Ceylon Observer Press, Colombo, 1872, p. 56.
34. *The Coffee Planter of Ceylon*, second edition, Colombo, 1870, pp. 76-77.

35. NAUK, CO, 54/476, No. 69 of 7 June 1872, see the private letter of Gregory to Herbert dated 10 June 1872; CO, 54/477, No. 59, letter of Gregory to Earl of Kimberley dated 9 July 1872.
36. NAUK, CO, 54/492, no. 7, letter of Gregory to Earl of Kimberley dated 8 January 1874.

Chapter - 6

Social Life of the Tamil Merchant Migrants, Exiled Convicts and Coolies in Malaya, 1786-1870

Tamil Muslim traders had migrated to the port of Melaka and lived there since the sixteenth century dominated by the European commercial activities in South East Asia. Many of them had made Melaka as their home and they were numerous and rose to positions of considerable power in the royal courts. Penang was only a transit point for small ships and part of the Kedah state but Tamil Muslims were present in the Island as early as 1786 before the arrival of the British.

Migration of Tamil Merchants and their Settlement in Penang

Tamil Muslim families had settled in Penang Island by 1786. Khader Moydeen *Marakkayar* had come with his brother called Muhammad Noorudin Marakkayar along with his mother. At that time Khader was 11 years old and his brother was aged 7. They left their native village of Parangi Pettai (Porto Novo) in Tamil country and on arrival in Penang started cloth business on family lines. When their textile business grew they travelled to Kedah, Aceh and other ports in South East Asia. Khader Moydeen and Muhammad Noorudin had developed their business so well in Penang that they had become successful cloth merchants and were the richest in the Island.[1]

The English East India Company when received Penang in 1786, the island had 158 Malays who were the inhabitants. The place was not of considerable significance in the long established intra-Asian maritime trade in the region. The English Company therefore tried its best to develop it as a colonial port-town for the purpose of gaining control of the Malay Straits. As a result, 154 new Malay settlers had arrived on the island within two years (by 1788). When Captain Francis Light founded the British settlement of Prince of Wales Island (i.e., Penang) with the establishment of the port of George Town on the island in 1786, many more Tamil traders and labourers arrived.[2] The British government appointed Khader Moydeen as head of the Indian Muslim community in Penang Island and in-charge of looking after the welfare, security and religion of the people at that time.

The opening of Penang by the British as a free trading port spurred the arrival of more Tamil Muslims, particularly the Javeed Periyannan (Jawi Peranakan) from Kedah. Earlier, after the fall of Melaka, Tamil Muslim traders had shifted their base to Kedah and a number of them got married and settled down.[3] The influx of Tamil Muslim migrants formed new settlements at Kampung Kolam, Lebuh Chulia and Jalan Masjid Kapitan Keling in the Island of Penang. According to the population statistics of August 1788 there were 216 Tamil immigrants and 121 Chinese in Penang.[4] This census does not include the European settlers and the number of Europeans working with the English company.

The expansion of the English colony of Penang in South East Asia created a demand for labour to construct public works like roads, harbour, offices, and jails. Convicts transported from Tamil country were planned to perform this labour as a substitute for the death penalty or long-term imprisonment. Penang came to emerge as a penal colony under the British when Cornwallis the Governor-General of India designated it in 1790 as the place for persons convicted of murder, robbery or other heinous offence sentenced by native courts in India to imprisonment for life, to which transportation was annexed by the British government. His instructions were to employ them in any manner, as long as it was consistent with the security of their persons, but to keep a watchful eye over them at all times, so as to prevent the possibility of their escape.[5] His successor, Wellesley the Governor-General continued its development as a penal site, although he expressed concern about its effectiveness, specifically its connections to Tamil Country from which it was about to receive convicts. He wondered whether it was a suitable place of banishment for prisoners from the Coromandel Coast because the place was resorted to by numerous trading vessels of the Tamil Muslims carrying on an extensive correspondence which might furnish the every means of returning to the place of their nativity to any the prisoners who were fortunate enough to escape from custody.[6]

Penang's reputation as a free trade port came to attract in the mean while a large number of settlers, and it gave adequate protection under the British flag. Maritime trade had developed in Penang and by 1793 George Town received 177 visits by significant ships. As early as 1794, the Straits Settlements Factory Records contain evidences of both the magnitude and the circularity of Tamil migration to the Melaka Straits, reporting that the vessels of the Coromandel Coast brought over annually 1,300 or 2,000 males who by traffic and various kinds of labour obtained a few dollars with which they returned to their homes.[7]

Penang's administration was headed by Francis Light (1786–94), the Superintendent. According to him, there were 1,500 to 2,000 Tamil Muslim immigrants in 1794 from the Coromandel Coast who came to Penang annually. However, most were sojourners who, after earning enough money, returned home.[8] Some Tamil Muslim merchants came to reside in Penang. It included Mohammed Syed and his partners, Mucktoon Sahib, Boojoo Mohammed and Ismail Mohammed hailing from Pulicat. They became wealthy merchants by trading in textiles and other goods. They had based their business in Penang from 1787 to 1814 till a fire destroyed all their properties.

By 1800, Penang became a home to 446 Indian convicts, from Bengal, Bombay and Madras, and by the time the Admiral Nelson docked in 1802 with its rebel prisoners, that number had grown to almost 600. In fact, Governor George Leith in Penang was eager to expand the convict population in 1800. In this respect, he echoed the views of his counterparts in many outposts of the British Empire, for whom convicts provided much needed labour literally and figuratively to help consolidate and develop their colonial settlements to alleviate the labour shortages that resulted from the decline after the abolition of the slave trade. There was much difficulty in recruiting local men and women in Malaya. The colonial administration in India conceived transportation of convicts as a means of deterring and reforming criminals through a punishment that sent them off to the growing number of British outposts, and more as a source of economic benefits because it provided labour. The governor of Penang had euphemistically termed it as a public service because the convict labour helped carry on public works.

In the development of Penang colony, the shortage of labour, both skilled and unskilled, was thought to be the real difficulty preventing the settlement from achieving the English East India Company's goals. Francis Light's importation of convict labourers from India and slaves from Bencoolen in

Sumatra helped to solve the unskilled labour shortage, but although George Town grew at an almost exponential rate, few skilled workers were attracted to Penang. George Leith the Governor wrote that the principal streets were properly raised and drained and the remainder had been then being finished. The town had in consequence improved much in appearance and cleanliness and it was reasonable to suppose would also be very healthy. The construction of regular streets and roads in the town area had been undertaken and completed leading to health improvement and prosperity in Penang.[9] Roads were extended three to four miles from Penang town, spreading from the most fertile and cultivated area of the island, a vital project consistent with administration policy to transform the colony into a spice producing area.[10]

By 1800 the number of ships visiting Penang had increased to 2,173. Many visits were repeat appearances of the sailing vessels of the country traders plying a regional trade, but, nevertheless, the statistics of Francis Light reflect an increasing inventory of shipping indicates, the harbour soon attracted numerous Tamil ships, Chinese junks and Malay *prahus* (boats). The harbour was deep enough, and close to shore, for ships to heave down using large jungle trees that grew right at the water's edge, the need for a dry dock and a careening-barge were not keenly felt. Under their auspices, thousands of Tamil Muslims arrived on Penang's shores each year, for a sojourn of months or years.[11]

It is reported that Tamil Muslims around 1500-2000 were found as seasonal traders and workers, of whom most of them came actually from the state of Kedah. These Tamil Muslims grew into an important community in Penang, as is evident from the foundation of the Kapitan Kling Mosque in 1801, and the Nagore *dargah* shortly afterwards. Tamil cultural forms and particularly forms of religious culture, travelled—or circulated—with the migrants. The *darghas* (shrines) to the saint of the Tamil town of Nagore, Shahul Hamid, on Chulia Street in Penang was built in 1801. It was the replica of the original *dargha* at the saint's burial place at Nagore. Tamil Muslims for the most part, maintained direct ties with the Coromandel Coast, exemplified by the construction of the Nagore *dargah*. This building dedicated to a Sufi saint was sponsored by the East India Company in Penang with a generous grant of land. The Capitan mosque at Pitt Street was built by the Kapitan of the Chulia, Khader Moydeen. Most of the Tamil Muslims used the Kapitan mosque as their major religious meeting place too.

Tamil Hindus also migrated to Penang and lived there since 1801. At around the same time, Hindus in the Island had erected the Murugan temple on the Penang Hill, then known as 'Gun Hill.' In 1801, the Company set land aside for a temple in George Town itself.

Exiled Convicts from Tamil Country to Penang and their Lives, 1802-25

The *paalayakkaarars* who challenged the authority of the English East India Company militarily were defeated in Tamil country and the end came in October 1801. Chinna Maruthu and Periya Maruthu of Sivagangai and Umaidurai were arrested. Seventy three of the principal rebels were also condemned for perpetual banishment. Among them were Vengum Periya Udaya Thevar of Sivagangi, Bomma Nayak of Verappur, Dalavai Kumarasamy Nayak of Panjalamkurichi and Durai Samy, the son of Maruthu Pandyan.

It is found mention in English Company records that the English had initially decided to ship the *paalayakaarars* of Tirunelveli and Ramanathapuram who were defeated in wars to Moluccas Islands, then under the British, because by that time the colonial Government in India had ruled out Botany Bay or the West Indies as penal destinations for the Indian convicts. However, with the change of affairs in Europe in 1802, the authorities realized that the Moluccas was no longer a viable option and therefore made plans to send them to Bencoolen in Sumatra. But that also did not happen because the commander of the ship who had been chartered in Bombay to transport them to Bencoolen refused to go there but agreed to sail to Penang.[12]

73 Convicts who were in Palayamkottai jail were taken to Tuticorin to board the ship 'Admiral Nelson' destined to Penang on 11 February 1802. James Welsh a British military officer who had fought against the *paalayakkaarars* in the wars was present at the scene of their departure from Tuticorin. His eyewitness account is remarkable because it is written in a sympathetic way. He stated his earlier friendship with the Maruthu brothers, especially Chinna Maruthu, who first taught him to throw the spear and he never failed to send James Welsh the presents of fine rice and fruit.[13] Charged with consigning the *paalayakaarar* prisoners to their armed escort on board the ship, Welsh had given a revealing glimpse into the emotions as they were on exile.

Welsh wrote that he had the combination of affection and despair which marked the fine countenance of his young friend Durai Samy, as he handed him into the boat. His companions in affliction displayed, on quitting their dear native land for ever. Welsh had the melancholy satisfaction of lightening the chains of Durai Samy, the younger and only surviving son of his former friend, Chinna Maruthu, a youth of about fifteen, condemned to perpetual banishment. With a mild and dignified resignation, the amiable young man bore his cruel fate without a murmur. As Durai Samy was consigned to the personal charge of James Welsh, to connive at his escape was impossible, but being under the same roof with him, in the large fortified factory, he was enabled to free him from his ignominious fetters, and separate him from the mass of his former menials. He was put up in a commodious chamber, enjoyed the company of his jailor and family, and fed with wholesome meals, dressed by a respectable man of his caste and religion.[14]

Lieutenant A. Rochead of the 2nd Battalion, 6th Regiment North India noted, that he had been directed to extend to them every practicable degree of lenity.[15] The voyage to Penang was something different for the rebel prisoners, for they had once enjoyed lives of privilege and status. It is interesting to note that Rochead was asked to explain why there had been casualties on board for he had received the men handcuffed in pairs with a pair of light irons connecting the alternate hands of two people and did not think it consistent with the discharge of his duty indiscriminately to lessen this restraint. In his opinion, a battalion of 20 men was not large enough to guard prisoners whom he characterized as having evinced that they possessed minds capable of a hazardous enterprise when their liberty was the object. Furthermore, he claimed that by the end of the voyage, nearly one third of the men were without handcuffs, beginning with six people whose irons he had struck off at the very outset of the voyage because he had appointed them to cook food for the rest. This arrangement was to ensure that dietary infractions were not committed on the high seas, an accommodation aimed at easing caste and religious concerns and a practice generally followed for Tamil soldiers who were required to cross the seas. As for their condition when they arrived in Penang and the three deaths, Rochead explained that much of what transpired stemmed from the extreme length of the voyage and not from anything he did that did not conform to the orders that he had been issued. There were many among his prisoners, he pointed out, who were old, infirm men and some in a bad state of health. Of the three who perished on the high seas, one was an old man who died of a bowel complaint. Another of a malady contracted on the ship that had no medical personnel on board. The third casualty was an old man who fell overboard.[16] Thus the prisoners who boarded the ship suffered miserably being kept under strict restraint and handcuffed with iron in pairs. The rest of the prisoners, 70 in number, reached Penang on 26 of April 1802 after the voyage for 76 days.

Soon after their arrival at the destination, one third of them fled in different directions. But their agony preyed upon them so much that 21 of them died within five months of banishment. Governor George Leith in Penang was much more apprehensive about having to contend with a large body of rebels. He also expressed his concern that they were so enfeebled and reduced as to be unable to walk when he first encountered them, and he even made sure to inform the Madras government that three deaths had occurred in transit and that the health of the surviving seventy prisoners was poor because of the real hardships they had suffered from want of water and to their being the whole time handcuffed.[17]

Leith told the authorities in India, these prisoners required careful watching, and he was not confident that he could do so with the troops he had on the island. Therefore, he eagerly awaited the arrival of two companies of marine battalions, which he believed had already been dispatched from India. As an added precautionary measure, he decided to locate his new prisoners beyond the pale of the burgeoning colony, in a hired house in the country.[18]

Leith described George Town in Penang was extensive, bounded to the north and east by the sea on the south by an inlet of the sea, called the Praingin river and on the west by the high road. The streets which crossed each other at right angles were spacious and airy; but had been at first merely lined out, without being either raised or drained, they were frequently impassable after hard rain, and at all times were dirty and filled with stagnant water.[19] Therefore Leith had decided and begun the practice of using more convicts as labourers and had requested the English Government in Calcutta to supply from India for constructing and maintaining the streets. The number of convicts employed in 1800 were 130, increasing to 772 by 1805. This cheap form of labour saved the budget.[20]

Governor Farquharson who succeeded Leith was also in favor of increasing his corps of convict workers. He claimed that he could engage as many as a thousand convicts in the docks only, and more in the other public works connected with the improvement of Penang. At that time, he had 772 convicts who were involved in various jobs such as plantations (80 convicts), making bricks for public works (100 convicts), cutting a canal and constructing an aqueduct (100 convicts), extending the pier into the sea from across the custom house (60 convicts), building and repairing the fortifications (60 convicts), building a new *sepoy* unit (50 convicts), scavenging (20 convicts), working in the marine yard and custom house (10 convicts), making roads (59 convicts), and working at the government house (30 convicts). There were, in addition, another 74 convicts who were incapable of work, 53 sick in hospital and 34 convalescents, and 43 men in irons because of their bad character. Eventually, his expectation was to assemble a convict labour force of 2,000 because these men were the best labourers in Penang and as the Company only paid for their provisions, their labour, even at the high estimation, cannot be half so expensive as that of hired labourers, who received each six dollars a month.[21]

Following the British occupation of Amboyna, thousands of pepper plants, as well as nutmeg, cinnamon, and clove trees were transplanted to Penang and distributed among the would-be planters. By 1805, the island was producing 2,000 tons of pepper, a valuable commodity which could be bartered for tea at Canton. Penang in 1809 had been described as a most convenient and desirable rendezvous, and place of refreshment to His Majesty's India squadron and to the numerous and valuable shipping engaged in the extensive trade carried on between the ports of Calcutta, Madras, and Bombay and China, the port of Manila, and other places of commercial resort in the eastern archipelago. It has been said that it was an entrepot for the merchandize of the East and West of India, and it afforded a ready and safe means for the barter of opium, piece goods, and other commodities of India, for the tin, rattans, betel nut and pepper of Malaya and these were also again being suited to the China market were there bartered for tea.[22]

With the development in the island and facilities that were offered the Tamil Muslims came to migrate from Kedah to Penang on a large scale and there were also Tamil Hindus and Muslims immigrants who came directly from the Coromandel Coast. They lived in a separate called Chulia street in Penang and had shops in Market Street. In Penang, new immigrant arrivals from the Coromandel Coast also encountered an already diverse South Asian population, which included East India Company soldiers and convict labourers from Madras and Bengal, as well as a large and growing number of Chinese migrants.[23]

It is gleaned from records that the *paalayakaarar* prisoners from Tamil country were never expected to do manual labor, and they resided apart from the convicts, who mostly lived and worked in and around town. They were initially lumped together with all the other prisoners from India who had been resettled in Penang. They all received the same ration of provisions and clothing which included 1 seer of rice per day per person, 1½ seers of salt per month, 1½ seers of ghee per month, and 1 piece of cloth per annum.

The lives of the *paalayakaarars* seemed to intersect with and parallel those of the convicts in some ways and to diverge in other ways. They sought to play up their differences by emphasizing their special status and circumstances. This insistence on their different and higher status was a refrain in their written requests, which consistently pressed for better living conditions and, ultimately, freedom to return home. In 1809 Durai Samy made a statement for the first time with a request for better conditions and it was granted. As he had completed seven years in exile, the shortest term of banishment for which convicts were transported and after which they were freed, he spoke at that hour publicly. By then, he and his fellow prisoners numbered only twenty-four; forty-nine of the original seventy-three had died. The Penang government agreed to make an exception in the case of Durai Samy so that he did not have to receive subsistence provided in kind, the way inferior prisoners were provisioned. Instead, he was to be given 20 Spanish dollars per month, his special treatment a reward, as one official put it. It was because for his exemplary conduct, the rank he bore in his own country prior to the disturbances, and his youth, which was taken to mean that he had not played a major role in the *paalayakaarar* wars.[24] In 1810, Auriatwa, had been described as a fifty-five-year-old person in bad health. He was afflicted with pains in his limbs and one side of his face swelled and disfigured. He was believed to escaped and had absconded by leaving on a native vessel that plied between Madras and Penang.[25]

Muslim and Hindu traders from Tamil country came to move over to Penang on a large scale and according to the official record of 1810, the largest ethnic groups of settlers in Penang were the Tamils with 5,604 in number and the Chinese were 5,088.[26] These were only the permanent residents of George Town and more people lived in outlying settlements on the island. There was a large itinerant population composed of soldiers, camp followers, mariners, and convicts.

Four years later, in 1814, a series of petitions were submitted, collectively and individually by the sixteen remaining Tamil convicts. Many of the petitions were signed in Telugu which was their mother tongue for they had settled in Tamil country during the period of Vijayanagara empire. A petition had the names of the former *paalayakkaars* affixed to it such as Aundookonda Vunnam Tirunelveli *zamindar* of Yail Avium Pannai Palayam, Ramaswamy Nayakkar, Samy *zamindar*, Kulaththur Vaulaswamy Nayakkar, Krishna Iyer Vitula *zamindar*; Paanjalam Ramaswamy, Puzhiyadi Paya Thevan. These petitions requested emancipation and return to Tamil country, a request seemingly prompted at that time by message they had received from the last vessels from the Tamil coast that many of their kinsmen in Madras had been released. The humble petition of Aundoo Konda Vunnam stated in an argument that several of his fellow prisoners could also have made that his exile had commenced when he was a young boy of about sixteen and did not have personal management of his *zamindar* and that he had been transported together with his uncle on his mother's side and the latter's minister, who he seemed to be the more culpable parties but who were then both dead. The two years he had been in confinement in Madras, followed by thirteen years on the Penang island, had lasted long enough to be deemed a sufficient expiation for the most serious transgression and the very extensive distress in particular he had experienced from the want of relatives and friends, torn from parents, possessions, and ease in his childhood, doomed to pass his youth in exile, for what it was hard to tell. He had little left in his life, as he could not take pride in a wife, a child, happiness or comfort all was far removed. Therefore, he pressed for a return to his parents and relatives.[27]

The Penang officials forwarded these petitions approvingly, highlighting in particular that the most considerable in rank were deceased, and that only sixteen now remain, who were either dependents upon their respective chieftains, or otherwise had but an inferior share in promoting the troubles. As they informed the Madras government, justice and humanity were on the side of these few remaining unhappy sufferers, whose general and individual behavior from the time of their arrival on the Penang Island had been characterized by regular, orderly, and peaceable demeanor. Separated as they were, from their friends, their families and their native country, added the Penang government, and with their country enjoying a state of tranquility and no apprehension existing of future trouble, it was natural for them to be desirous of returning to the coast.[28] Nevertheless the petitions were denied, except that of Krishna Iyer.

The survivors of the former *paalayakaaras* were not allowed to return, largely because of the response of the Tirunelveli magistrate, who felt obligated first to recount the violent events of the two rebellions that led to the banishment. Although sanguine about any new challenges to the authority of government, he expressed some concern about what effect the return of the prisoners would have on the many naturally turbulent people who were currently without means of support and who had formerly backed the *paalayakaarar* rebels. He also noted and this point was intended to be alarming that the petitioners, if allowed to return, would be coming back to a district where they formerly enjoyed both affluence and authority and where they would be faced with a situation in which their lands had been sold or given to other *paalayakaarars*. Finding themselves in such a degraded situation, they would, he opined, consider any change advantageous and having nothing to risk but the loss of life, on which class of people set but little value, would do everything in their power to set on foot another rebellion.[29]

In 1815, in the following year the prisoners once again made their appeals, and this time they noted that Krishna Iyer had been freed and he had returned to the Tamil coast. They also emphasized that a banishment of fourteen years could not be just considered as a light punishment even for atrocious crimes. They spoke up on this occasion that fourteen years, after all, represented the number of years in exile that God Rama had served as found in the great epic of Ramayanam in Hinduism. The convicts drew on the themes of good and evil, and stories of exile and of Lanka (Ceylon), the island capital of the evil demon Raavana appealing especially to prisoners and convicts transported to different islands across the ocean. In fact, convicts, regardless of where they were transported to, often considered their penal settlements to be their Lanka.[30]

The petitioners also pressed for terms designed to further differentiate themselves from the convicts in case release was not forthcoming. They put it, that they needed a more generous stipend, which was only 6 dollars per month right then and which was not more than the wages of common labourers.[31] Subsequent petitions continued to speak in the idiom of emancipation and concessions. Their requests seeming to press more insistently mentioning that they had been strongly denied in 1814 because of the objections of the Magistrate of Tirunelveli.

In 1817 the convicts repeated their pleadings for augmentation in their stipends or pensions, as they once referred to these allowances, as if they were receiving a salary for having prior service to government had led the local authorities to grant them a monthly stipend of 15 dollars each.[32] Coincidentally, their 1818 request for an increase of 1 dollar in stipend in lieu of clothing was approved by J. A. Bannerman, who had waged war against them as an officer in the Madras Army and who in 1817 had become the governor of Penang. In his new capacity, he turned very kind towards the 12 paalayakaarars.[33] That year, the surviving prisoners also encountered James Welsh whom they had known earlier fought alongside Bannerman who had escorted them from Palayamkottai Jail to Tuticorin to board the ship Admiral Nelson to Penang.

Welsh's account of 1818 provides a revealing glimpse. He said that he received a sudden visit from a miserable decrepit old man whom when he demanded his name and business, looked for some time at his face, the tears ran down his furrowed cheek, and at length he uttered the word Durai Samy. It came like a dagger to the heart of James Welsh. This poor young prisoner stood before him, dreadfully changed in outward appearance, but still with the same mind, and cherishing the remembrance of former days and former friendships. The casual hearing of his name had revived affection, and, he much feared, the mistaken hope, that an advancement in rank might afford him the convicts, by contrast, primarily received rations in kind and a tiny amount of money to buy bazaar necessaries.[34] These were valued at a little over 2 dollars per convict means of lessening his misery. Durai Samy even entreated Welsh to be the bearer of letters to his surviving family, but this he understood was contrary to the existing orders; since, though he found the Governor of Penang, the late Colonel Bannerman, his former commanding officer, kind and considerate, it did not appear to rest with him, and Welsh was compelled to decline.[35] Welsh hoped that the directors of the English East India Company would alleviate the sufferings of an innocent man by releasing him because the Tamil country was then completely settled, and there was no chance of any ill effects, as regards state policy, likely to accrue from such a compassionate measure.[36]

The authorities in London had finally decided to release the prisoners by August 1818. Deliberations held at the highest level of government, the Board of Control, essentially sided with the claims that the *paalayakaarars* had been articulating for many years. The Board of Control echoed the longstanding assertions of the petitioners that they had been young men when they were seized, that they had not been actively involved in the rebellion, and that the survivors were mostly of lower rank. In the Board's words, the petitioners at those periods must have been under the absolute control of their parents, and could not therefore, without injustice, be considered as participating in their guilt, yet they had been subjected to the same rigorous punishment, and made, as too truly stated in the words above quoted from one of the petitions, to expiate offences not their own. Continuation of their exile, it observed, would therefore be in a high degree unjust. Thus, its directive was that they be permitted to return to reside with their relatives or such of them as still survived, and that there be granted to each of them, either in land or in a pecuniary stipend, at his option, an allowance or provisions adequate to his liberal support, together with any other marks of kindness that the Governor of Penang shall judge best calculated to fulfill the intentions. The Board's letter also referred to the recent release in Madras of the relatives of Umaidurai, which, in its view, made it all the more difficult to justify their residence as prisoners in Penang. Clearly, there was no danger in allowing their return. The letter had put that there was no rational grounds for apprehending that the Company's authority would be weakened or endangered by the return of a few obscure individuals whose conduct, moreover, during the exile years, had been orderly regular and inoffensive. Whether their banishment was originally just and expedient, the Board of Control chose not to expand on, except by stating that it believed their suffering had satisfied all the ends both of justice and policy.[37]

It is known that Durai Samy had passed away in the meantime. The Madras authorities concurred that it was safe to allow them to return because of the present settled state of the country. When J. M. Coombs, the officer who had been in-charge of them since 1812 and who considered their uniform conduct, correct and satisfactory in every particular had informed them of their release. But the convicts also used this occasion to seek permission to take their ten followers, whom they had obviously acquired during their stay, with them.[38] Their return, however, as with their years in exile, required further negotiations. This involved seeking the opinion of the magistrate of Tirunelveli and the Madras government. With the magistrate refusing to allow the remaining seven convicts back into his district, the only option was to find other locales to house them. One option offered was Chingleput, which lay a considerable distance to the north in Tamil country and was close to the seat of government, the city of Madras, from which the authorities were presumably better positioned to keep a watchful eye over them. Six of the prisoners expressed willingness to accept the government offer, although not before countering by suggesting their relocation to Tiruchirapalli on the grounds that they would, from there, have opportunities of seeing their relatives because it was closer to their native place but did not state the fact in writing. Aundookonda Vunnam was the sole holdout and he refused to stay at Chingleput as an acceptable venue and he cited Madurai as the place where he was willing to go.[39] The matter was solved in the beginning by sending them back to Madras. The convicts released had been living in Chingleput under the custody of peons. In 1825, almost after a quarter century, the surviving five convicts were granted permission to return to Tirunelveli. They were required to reside in a house found by government, subsist on a government-authorized daily allowance, function on a daily basis in the custody of peons, go about only if accompanied by a peon, and stay put in the house appropriated to them during the night.[40] Thus the life of the exiled convicts from Tamil Country to Penang and return to Tirunelveli had been found to be very miserable.

The Tamil population in the town of Penang in due course of time had decreased and in 1818 it had 4844 Tamils out of the total population of 12,135 persons. Interestingly we find the break-up details. Accordingly there were 1,043 males and 162 females who were below 14 years, 3098 males and 379 females between 15-39 years and 116 males and 46 females more than 40 years. Thus the Tamil males represented 26% of the overall population while the females were just 3%.[41] It may be pointed out that during an outbreak of cholera in 1819 the government requested the assistance of the chief of the Tamil Muslim community to explain the disease to the community in order to help curb its spread.[42]

By the 1820s, Tamil settlers constituted the largest single group in George Town, the urban settlement in Penang Island. A number of court cases throughout the period show the involvement of Tamil Muslims in shipping who had been found as owners, captains, and officers of trading vessels.[43]

Tamil population had increased in the meanwhile to 4996 in 1822 and it represented the biggest ethnic group with 36.25 per cent of the total population of Penang.[44] Thus Tamils remained the highest from 1818 to 1822 pushing the Chinese to the second place. The total population of the Island according to the census of 1833 had been 40,300. While 789 Europeans, 21 Armenians and 708 native Christians had been recorded the population of Tamils had been unknown.[45] Penang was reduced to a presidency by the British while Singapore was declared as the headquarters of the Straits Settlements in 1830. This in a way reduced the importance of Penang and also affected its growth in the future.[46]

With the building of the temple dedicated to the Goddess Maariamman in Queen Street in 1833 the Hindus began to celebrate their festival of Thaipusam. It was an annual celebration in honor of God Murugan, son of Siva and Parvathi commemorating his defeat of Itumpan on Palani Hill. Observing Thaipusam in Penang in 1834 James Low, the chief military officer of Province Wellesley, wrote that when people had forsaken their own country in Tamil country and voluntarily settled in Penang they were satisfied with the permission to celebrate their religious rites only which did not outrage the proper feelings of the other portions of the community, and these were not injurious to public morals, the decencies of life, and order.[47]

Immigration of Tamil Coolie Labourers from Karaikal, Nagore, Nagapattinam and Madras to Penang and their Lives, 1848-1870

The years 1848-9 saw an increase in the number of sailing voyages between Penang and the Tamil coast. To English observers, the Tamil connection with the straits of Melaka appeared entirely natural, and governed by the trading networks.[48] Nevertheless, the sheer number of ships conducting the voyages elicited official concern, because for the past seven years since 1842 migration began to feature prominently from the port of Karaikal. A number of cases came to light in which seriously overcrowded native vessels began to arrive at Penang. An observer wrote in 1848, wrote that it was notorious to find the crowded manner in which the sailing vessels arrived with coolies at Penang, and the consequences in that year had been very fatal, that many of the passengers died en route.[49] Regulations, however, appeared an impossibility and so dispersed was the trade and traffic, from small as well as large ports on the Tamil coast. It was felt that if regulations were tightened in Penang, ships wishing a passage could readily embark to other ports on Malay coast.[50] The Hindu and Muslim shipping merchants had constituted the essential link between the port cities of the Melaka Straits and Tamil country. They advanced to thousands of labourers the cost of their passage overseas, and linked them up with the estate employers in Penang.[51] In 1848, at an estimate, 2,700 passengers had arrived in Penang from the ports of Tamil country. This number had swelled and risen to around 6,000 passengers during 1860.[52]

According to records, Tamils had sailed and migrated from the port of Karaikal under the French East India Company in ships that sailed to Penang. In November 1850 the ship Maureau Fils had sailed away from Pondicherry. Again the ship Le Verrie took 80 coolies and there was a medical inspection of the labourers to prevent death on board who sailed at that time.[53] A price of ten rupees had been paid and these coolies arrived in Penang.

Labourers had on a large scale migrated from the French territory of Karaikal. It is reported that 10,370 migrants were exported between 1856 and 1860. There were 2533 coolies embarked in 1852 and it is noted exclusively that an account of 344 persons hailed from Karaikal.[54]

In the ship to Penang in 1857 there travelled 295 men, 10 women and 19 children from Karaikal totaling 324 persons. In 1858 we find mention of 3291 out of 3383 in total had migrated from Karaikal to Penang. In October 1859 Durand d' Ubraye the French Governor gave clear signals for migration. Therefore in 1859 we find 989 labourers had sailed for

Penang.[55] Again in 1861 we find 120 labourers had sailed away in a ship that reached Penang.[56]

Labour recruitment was conducted and the workers mainly came from the hinterland of the ports of Nagore and Nagapattinam but they boarded the ship at Karaikal where they had been reported in the French records as coolies for migration. No written contracts were also made in some cases and it was very difficult to establish by proof that these coolies were taken for what could be the exact and express purpose. The migration had increased from Karaikal and the French administration derived large revenue at the port which was around 1553 francs.

The migration of Coolies from Karaikal to Penang, 1850-62

Year	*Number of migrants*
1850	298
1851	571
1852	3296
1854	3136
1855	2763
1856	1003
1857	513
1858	564
1859	3383
1860	1467
1861	604
1862	1036
Total	**18634**

Source: Roucaia Badat, *Un Comptoir Francais des Indes: Karaikal de 1850 a 1862*, Memoire de Maitrise d' Histoire, Universite de Aix-en-Provence, 1972, pp. 111-2.

The British became obsessed with migration from Karaikal in French India to Penang evading British control. Standing at the margins, outside the boundaries of British India, these officials reflected on the weaknesses in the law. The emigrant from Karaikal was given a passport from the local police, which had been granted to him as a French subject. Indenture was more important in the labour recruitment from Tamil country to Malaya. Under this an employer working to recruit immigrants would engage one of the labour recruitment firms in Tamil country or send agents to Tamil coast to recruit labourers directly. The agents advanced money to those who were ready to migrate to Malaya. The advance was cardinal on the intending migrants for signing a contract. They were then deemed to be under indenture to their employer for a fixed period varying from minimum three to maximum five years. They could not change either employer or a place of employment. When their period of indenture was completed they could be re-indentured for a further period or released from indenture, provided they had paid off the expenses incurred in their recruitment. Though wages were fixed at the time of recruitment it was in reality subject to change. The charges for recruitment and the expenses involved in the transport of labour were borne by the employer and the wages calculated after deducting this initial outlay.

When large scale migration took place from the French port of Karaikal it worried the British. Therefore the Indian Act of 1857 was introduced and in 1859 the British Crown established regulations for the movement of ships which came into force to prevent the abuse of transporting large number of coolies. By the end of the 1860s, the Chief Secretary of the Straits Settlements observed that there was a large scale regular coolie migration from the Tamil coast to Penang. Many ships belonging to Hindus and Muslims were employed in it, and the number of persons who are thus brought over was believed to average 4,000 per annum. Almost all the boatmen, caulkers, and labourers in the port town of Penang,—syces, watermen, and a large number of hawkers, traders and domestic servants, were hailing from the Tamil coast.[57]

By 1867 there was, however, a great deal of cultural mixing with Tamils and Malays. It is reported in Penang, that a hybrid, localized variant of the Shi'a Muharram procession came to be observed and it also came to attract Sunni Muslims. In 1867 Penang Riots broke out and it had also involved rival alliances and brotherhoods that cut across the lines of community and religion.[58]

W. L. Hathaway, the sub-collector of Thanjavur district in 1870 voiced against the traffic and large scale migration of people overseas from the port of Nagapattinam to Penang. He alleged that migration was a regularly organized system of kidnapping. Time and again, the captives were shipped from Nagapattinam to Penang, where the males were employed as coolies, and the females sold to a life of prostitution. Hathaway wrote that the migration was contrary to the Act XIII of 1864. He said that the law had made it illegal to assist any native of India in emigrating. He insisted the Madras government to take adequate steps and intervene to stop the coolie traffic. He wrote in this connection to the Journal titled 'Friend of India' read by British and Indian critics of imperial policy and embarrassed the authorities. He pleaded and pursued the ship-owners and labour contractors in Nagapattinam not to indulge in such activities. At the start of the emigration season in 1870, he ordered a raid on a warehouse where the migrants waited to board ships for Penang. They were brought before the local magistrate. It was found at that time that each migrant mentioned that he had acted according to his own free will. The young boys declared that the labour recruiters were their fathers, uncles and close relatives and so they had not signed at all any contracts which were not required. Hence there was no evidence that they were all migrating for the purposes of coolie labour. Hathaway sadly noted that it was useless to make a sincere attempt to unravel the real facts of the case of migration when the people themselves did not reveal the truth.[59] Hathaway had thus described the illegal traffic in people to Penang with two overlapping concerns. The first was the humanitarian anxiety that these people were being kidnapped, enslaved, or otherwise taken against their will. The second was that the trafficker was functioning like a pirate and he was independent of the British control.

The sugar planters in the Wellesley province in Malaya adopted the indenture system of labour recruitment where the passage costs were recovered from the labourers within two years from their wages. Though they could not be compelled to pay under the law, given the low wages it was extremely difficult to pay back and in the process got caught up in the cycle of indebtedness. Under the *kangaani* system the debt-bondage condition of labourers persisted. Therefore we have no statistics available for most of the labourers who had migrated to Penang by trips back home or constant stream of returning back to Tamil country.

Much of the coolie trade appears to have been carried out by Tamils themselves employing Tamils-owned sailing ships till 1870s. When British shipping regulations and migration controls at Nagapattinam became very stringent, the Tamil Muslim shipping merchants did as their predecessors had done and simply set sail from the adjacent French port of Karaikal. However, ships also had set sail from Nagapattinam to Penang carrying coolies. A local Police Weekly Circular had reported the case. On finding a warehouse full of coolies crowded together like beasts, the police superintendent refused to let their ship depart from Nagapattinam. Questioning the detained men, the police official found that the coolies had got their stories and all of them had answered satisfactorily enough. They also produced details of parents, uncles, or guardians. The superintendent thought, that this coolie trade had reached such a large dimension that there was plenty of room for an Emigration Agent. This goal was finally secured only in 1873, when a protector of emigrants was appointed to oversee migration to Southeast Asia.[60]

While migration of coolies to Penang from Tamil coast though continued on a large scale, we find W.J. Hathaway, the sub-collector of Nagapattinam denounced on 12 March 1870 the coolie trade to Penang as illegal. The emigration was totally suspended in June 1872 vide Act XIV of 1872. The protector of emigrants totally stopped the emigration from Nagapattinam.[61] However, W.T. Davidson the officer in Madras opined that the Tamil region under the French and the English was an overpopulated country and there could be little difficulty in inducing any number of people to emigrate to Penang overseas.[62]

The fundamental shift in patterns of migration and the capitalist development in the plantations in Malaya developed with the establishment of British control over most of the area by 1870. The west coast of Malaya was opened to European capital, and to considerable investments in coffee plantations, followed late by rubber in the nineteenth century. Unable to attract or coerce local Malay labour, and without access to the networks controlling Chinese labour, European planters looked across the Tamil coast for the supply of workers.[63] Lacking significant access to Chinese labour throughout the planters had to recruitment of workers from Tamil country. Moreover the Chinese labour was found to be expensive. The straits settlement personal status was closed in 1873 and convicts were removed to the Andaman Island.

The categorical distinction between coolies who migrated under agreement to labour, and free migrants, whose travels within the British Empire had been unregulated. It caused further problems for those charged with law enforcement. The emigration of Indians to Straits Settlements was actually declared illegal and it was prohibited by Act XIII of 1864. However, strict restrictions came to be placed on emigration to Penang from the Tamil coast in 1867 when Malaya was separated from India. The Straits Settlements ordinance of no.1 also known as the Indian Immigrants Protection Ordinance of 1876 or the Indian Act No. 5 of 1877 was applied. It subsequently governed the indentured labour migration and the wages came to be fixed at 12 cents a day and not more than 1 pound in any one month could be deducted in respect of advances. No coolie labourer was allowed to work for more than six days a week. Not more than 10 hours was to work a day or more than 6 hours without a break. The exploitation of the coolie workers in the past had necessitated in introducing some legal remedies. Coolies from Tamil country had migrated to work in the coffee and rubber plantations after 1880.

Migration of Tamils to Singapore and their Social Life, 1809-70

Sir Stamford Raffles obtained the Island of Singapore from the Sultan of Johor and the British established themselves there in 1809.[64] This happened after 23 years of the foundation of Penang. Raffles refers to the presence of Tamil Muslims after the founding of the English settlement in Singapore.[65] It is mentioned that a certain ship belonged to some Muslim merchants from Nagore was found at Singapore harbour while the ship owner's name was Ganapathi *chetti*, a Hindu.[66]

The piracy in the sea of Melaka Straits was a problem to the ships and sailors. On 7 June 1823, Raffles wrote John Crawford, the new Resident of Singapore that piracy in the Melaka Straits had become so common and frequent that the square-rigged vessels of the Tamil Muslims are precluded from coming further than Penang or Aceh, and so the trade of fifty or sixty brigs and ships are lost to Singapore.[67] Raffles thus had noted the losses Singapore incurred because the ships of the Tamil Muslims avoided Singapore for fear of piracy. In a report of 1824 by Crawford we find mention of Tamil Hindus who traded with Singapore and he made exclusive mention of them as respectable as traders.[68] Tamil Muslims in Singapore made their living not by trade, but also by undertaking various jobs in the employment of others. The British town-planners had observed the Chulia Campong (Tamil Muslim quarters) which was to be at a location where their services are most likely to be called for.[69] Further the Chulia Muslim and Dhoby (washermen) encampment near the Sepoy Lines was also removed in the year 1823.[70] The boundary between boatmen and dockworkers had been porous, and the noisy Tamil Hindus who manned the cargo-boats had also loaded and unloaded the cargoes.[71]

An important change was effected in 1826 by the British when Singapore, Melaka and Penang became known collectively as the Straits Settlements, with Singapore as the administrative centre. The population according to a census taken on 1 January 1827 in Singapore, there were 209 males, 53 women amounting to a total of 262 natives of Bengalis. We find 772 males and 7 women who were Tamils amounting to a total of 779. Thus among the Indians, Tamils population had been large in number.[72] Singapore began to develop since 1832 when it replaced Penang as capital of the Straits Settlements. In 1839 we find mention of a race of Malay sampans generally manned by the Tamil Hindu boatmen in Singapore. We find also the mention of both the Tamil Hindu and Muslim boatmen in the Singapore Free Press.[73]

Tamil Muslims involved in shipping business and worked as lightermen, wharfingers, and owners of cargo-boats in Singapore. There is considerable evidence for Tamil Muslims owning and letting out cargo-boats and tongkangs too.[74] The importance of business activities by Tamil Muslims in Singapore is noted from sources. Trade in cloth had been a mainstay of the Tamil Muslims and in 1855, a Malay resident of Singapore complained about the fraudulent practices adopted at the cloth shops by the Tamil Hindus. It is recorded that the Malays and the Bugis were tricked into buying low-quality cloths in near darkness.[75] These shops had been also rather small, and they carried on both the wholesale and retail business in textiles. Tamil Muslims not only shipped commodities between Tamil Coast and Singapore, they also had their own establishments and shops in Singapore. In 1843, complaints were lodged about Tamil Hindus blocking the verandahs with their goods in many places.

The population details of Tamil migrant Hindus and Muslims in Singapore in 1849 by Turnbull is important for it shows that thirty years after the foundation of Singapore, the Tamil Muslims had clearly outnumbered their Hindu compatriots. There were 4915 Tamil Muslims and 1346 Tamil Hindus who made a total of 6,261 while the Muslims formed 78.5%, of the population.[76] The same census also referred to only 17 merchants out of the population for it had actually lumped the merchants together with clerks and this prevents us from drawing general conclusions from the figures. It should also be noted that the majority of the Tamils around 42.8% appear in the 'miscellaneous' section, and it gives us from gaining somewhat a neat picture of economic activity of the Tamils in Singapore at that time. Thus in the census of 1849, we notice that the labourers had made up around 40% of all working Tamils and most of them have been Muslims.[77]

In 1851, the Straits Settlements were placed under the direct control of the Governor-General of India to reduce the financial expenditure of the administration. Due to much agitation from local merchants and British officials, the Straits Settlements, along with Labuan (ceded to the British in 1846) were separated from India in 1867. They were then administered directly by the Colonial Office in London. It has been mentioned by this time (in 1866) that the Tamil Muslims had been an affluent community in Singapore.[78] Further, the common occupation of Tamil Hindus and Muslims was mentioned that of syce, i.e. a groom looking after draft-horses. Several

Tamil Muslim syces are also found mention on the pages of the Singapore Free Press in 1866.[79] Indeed, the owners of carriages were frequently Tamils.[80] Some of them were very famous and including 'Butler Masthan', the butler of the governor of Singapore in the 1870s, who hailed Mutlur near Chidambaram in Tamil country. Tamils had worked as office peons. The Singapore Free Press had also referred to office Tamby.[81] It is noticed that a few Tamil Muslims seem to have worked as translators and clerks for the British courts and lawyers.[82] The names mentioned include Hajee Saffer Ally and his delinquent son Akbar Ally besides Mohammad Gouse.[83] *Dubash* Mohamed a Tamil had been mentioned in the record of 1866.[84] Thus the Tamil Muslims in Singapore were of various kinds like unskilled workers, traders and also employed as salesmen in the shops of others.[85]

Temples Built and Festivals Celebrated: The Social and Religious Customs of the Hindu Tamils in Singapore

In 1827, Narayana *pillai*, a Tamil building contractor who arrived in Singapore with Sir Stamford Raffles, the founder of the British settlement erected the Sri Maariamman Temple on a piece of land granted by the English East India Company authorities.[86] In a petition we find that the English company had granted a sufficient ground for the occupation, and also for the Church, near the banks of the Fresh Water River, and accordingly observed that place, and built the houses and a Church. Maariamman Temple was built in immediate proximity to another place of worship. The temple's sacralization of the land in terms of Hindu cosmology bordered upon the largest Tamil Muslim mosque, the Masjid Jamae, which indicated a parallel connection. Therefore as early as in 1827, a dispute arose between the trustees of the mosque and the temple and use of the public road located in between.[87]

The British colonial government in Singapore was always wary of the processions in the town and their potentially disturbing character. As early as in 1842, it refused to allow the religious processions to the Hindus. Hence they went on a short strike on that account. However, the processions were apparently resumed after seven years and in 1849 the Grand Jury claimed that processions were allowed to the Hindus and Indian convicts, but they were not to be taken out in public streets. However, the Chinese were forbidden to take out processions and banned completely.

Decades later, in 1860, the trustees of the Maariamman Temple in Singapore desired to celebrate *theemithi* (a fire-walking Hindu ceremony) in honor of Draupathi, wife of the Pandava brothers in the Mahabharata.

They were denied permission to perform the rites of *theemithi* in public, the Governor's Council declaring it their responsibility to prevent the peace of the town being in any way disturbed.[88]

Mosques Built and Festivals Celebrated: The Social and Religious Customs of the Tamil Muslims in Singapore

A mosque was founded by Tamils called the Masjid Jamae and it was established in 1826-27. The Masjid Al-Abrar was established in 1827, on the original mosque on the site where the Masjid Malabar is located nowadays. A *dargah* in Singapore was built between 1828 and 1830 in Telok Ayer Street, then almost directly on the seashore and it is a replica of Tamil town of Nagore the famous shrine, to the saint Shah al-Hamid (Shahul Hamid). The Masjid Abdul Gafoor in Singapore was established in the year 1859. Tamil Muslims celebrated important religious functions and festivals. On 5 February 1857, during the annual festival of Shah al-Hamid, a small riot at the intersections of Telok Ayer Street and Boon Tat Street (then Japan Street), left two people dead in Telok Ayer Street overzealous police inspector tried to remove obstructions in the shape of stakes and plantain trees stuck in the ground to the chagrin of the Tamil Muslims.[89]

Tamil Muslims also celebrated Muharram festival in Singapore. A conflict that broke out during Muharram processions led to banning the festival procession in 1864.[90] In Singapore by that time the Muharram processions had become apparently the preserve of two groups of Indian Muslims secret societies, while one with the white flags and the other with the red flags. The two group processions were strictly monitored and kept apart, while the white flags usually went first on their circuit through the business district and China-Town. In the year 1864 a serious incident happened during the procession that members of the red flags society entered the building and destroyed things. Owing to this disturbance the court in 1866 made banning of the practice of Muharram processions. After that the processions were stopped completely.[91] The British Indian government officials felt embarrassment and annoyance on the large scale migration of the Tamils, and so the Supreme Court of Singapore confirmed in 1878 that migrants from Karaikal and Pondicherry in French India were excluded from the laws governing migration between India and the Straits.

Conclusion

Tamil workers were recruited either as assisted or unassisted labour. Under the category of assisted there were two types of recruitment systems indenture and *kangaani*. The distinctive feature of the history of Tamil experience in the Malay Peninsula lies in the character of the port cities of Penang and Singapore. Both the port towns were more open, more cosmopolitan, with a greater mixture of peoples and languages, than almost any other land to which Tamils moved. Coolie trade with Malaya, though illegal as per the Indian law under Act XIII of 1864, it had flourished and was very profitable for ship-owners. With the grant of formal permission in 1872, immigration to Malaya came to be controlled under regulatory devices of license recruiting, inspection of depots and registration of recruits. With British colonial state intervention and the arrival of steam, however, European shipping companies took over the indentured traffic between Tamil Coast and Malaya. The planters procured their labour from Tamil country through British companies based in Madras who worked with a network of local *maistry* recruiters. Tamil labour recruitment for the coffee and rubber plantations in Malaya from 1876-77 onwards was solely carried out at Nagapattinam and Madras by the Government of the Straits Settlements. A system of licensing of *kangaanis* was introduced. The license forms were filled out at the plantations with details of name of the *kangaani*, his commission, the permissible number of recruits and wage rates etc. From the plantations they proceeded to Penang or Port Swettenham, registered their license and embarked for India. On arrival in India their licenses were endorsed by Malayan Emigration Agent at two Malayan emigration depots. One functioned at Avadi near Madras and another at Nagapattinam. After completing these formalities the *kangaanis* went to the financial agents of their employers–M/S Binny & Company or M/S Madura Company–and received an advance of Rs 20 for travel and recruiting expenses. Most of the *kangaani* recruits were from the districts of Chingleput, North Arcot, South Arcot and Salem to transport the coolies to Avadi and from there they were sent in ships from Madras. *Kangaanis* recruited coolies from Tiruchirapalli and Thanjavur were taken to Nagapattinam and boarded ships after completing the formalities of checking licenses and conducting medical examinations etc. He paid their fares from a lump sum advanced by the employer. The recruited Indian immigrant labourers entered Malaya at Penang, which was the only entry port that functioned (until 1903). When all restrictions to Indian emigration to Malaya were removed only in 1897, we find the *chettiar* and *lebbai* Tamil Muslim merchants did their own recruiting and they advertised their services openly in the Penang press. One such firm was M. Ganapathi Pillai & Company, announced in the 'Penang Standard' that any gentleman requiring the services of Indian agricultural labourers could be supplied with any number of men of strong and sound constitution at moderate brokerage and within a reasonable time after notice. Further in the period of 1880s we find the Spanish vessel *Zamboga* and the German ships *Septima* and *Decima* were all regular visitors to Karaikal, and the substitution of these foreign steamers entirely removed the captains and crews of these vessels from the moral influence of British consular authority. Labour migration to all the eleven states of peninsular Malaya that took place must be understood properly in the later periods. The expansion of commercial agriculture especially in coffee and rubber necessitated and enlarged labour supply and conditions of service. Thus the system of labour recruitment to Penang for sugar plantations had got gradually expanded but it was totally different from the period from 1849 to 1876. As the English East India Company's monopoly came under increasing political pressure, Singapore enjoyed a unique status, being an almost completely free port under the aegis of the Company's exclusive rights. Not surprisingly, Singapore's growth was more dramatic than Penang's had been, but although many predicted the complete destruction of Penang, this was not to be. True, the centre of gravity of British interests in South East Asia shifted to the southern end of the Straits of Melaka, but Penang retained a share of its former trade and adjusted well to the challenge posed by Singapore, becoming the hub of its own regional trade network rather than the unsuccessful rival of Raffles' new colony.

The formation of the Straits Settlements in 1826, and the eventual transfer of the capital to Singapore in 1832 were blows to Penang, but they were not fatal ones. No longer relying on the English Company's ships, or even on the China trade, the colony adapted to a more dynamic, less monolithic socio-economic order, and even to changing political conditions. Singapore was under Indian rule from 1826 to 1867 (Eastern Presidency of the British-India Government). The Indian rule in Singapore was terminated in 1867. Tamil Migrants in Singapore were said to be sailors, traders and office employees between 1809 and 1878. They were both Hindus and Muslims and they came to follow the socio-religious customs prevalent in Tamil country in India.

Notes

1. Eusoff, Ragayah, *The Merican Clan: A Story of Courage and Destiny*, Times Books International, 1997.
2. T. J. Newbold, *Political and Statistical Account of the British Settlements in the Straits of Malacca*, 2 vols., London, 1839, see vol. 1.
3. Eusoff, Ragayah, *The Merican Clan: A Story of Courage and Destiny*, Times Books International, 1997.

4. British Library (hereafter BL), London, Oriental and India Office Collection (hereafter OIOC), Straits Settlements: Factory Records (hereafter SSFR), G/34/3.
5. 'Francis Light, Fort Cornwallis, 25th January 1794', in, Journal of the Indian Archipelago and Eastern Asia (hereafter JIAEA), vol. 5, 1851, p. 9.
6. BL, Board's Collection (hereafter BC), India, 1798/99-1825/26, OIOC, F/4/825, 21910 to 21927, BC, 1825-26, Cornwallis letter dated 11 March 1790, cited in extract of 15 April 1824.
7. BL, F/4/142, 2489, BC, 1802, Wellesley to Clive dated 17 August 1802.
8. Arkib Negara Malaysia, Kuala Lumpur, Microfilm of Straits Settlements Factory Records, vol. 6 (1794) to vol. 13 (1806); see also, BL, OIOC, G/34/6, SSFR, vol. 6, 1794, see 1 August 1794.
9. George Leith, *A Short Account of the Settlement, Produce and Commerce of Prince of Wales Island in the Straits of Malacca*, London, J. Booth, 1805, p. 24.
10. BL, OIOC, G/34/4, See the minutes and resolution of the Boards of Trade on Captain Light's letter, at Fort William, dated 14 January 1790.
11. John Crawford, *History of the Indian Archipelago: Containing an Account of the Manners, Arts, Languages, Religions, Institutions and Commerce of Its Inhabitants*, 3 vols., Edinburgh, 1820, see vol. 1.
12. Cleveland Public Library, Ohio, USA, MS East India Company, 1807, Report on the Origin, Progress and Termination of the Poligar Wars in the Southern Provinces.
13. James Welsh, *Military Reminiscences: Extracted from a Journal of Nearly Forty Years' Active Service in the East Indies*, London, Smith, Elder, 1830, p. 130.
14. James Welsh, Military Reminiscences, pp. 133-34.
15. BL, BC, 1803-04, extract of Rochead letter, Fort St. George, Military, no. 2737.
16. BL, BC, 1803-04, F/4/155 (2965 to 2744), 2737, letter of Rochead to government dated 8 March 1803-04.
17. BL, BC, 1803-04, F/4/155, 2737, See the letter of Leith to government.
18. Ibid.
19. George Leith, A Short Account of the Settlement, p. 24.
20. Kernial Singh Sandhu, 'Tamil and other Indian Convicts in the Straits Settlements AD. 1790–1873', *Proceedings of the First International Conference of Tamil Studies*, Kuala Lumpur, 1968, vol. 1, pp. 197–208.
21. BL, Bengal Public Consultations (hereafter BPC), 1805, P/6/12, letter of R. T. Farquharson to government, dated 15 March 1805, 16 May 1805 and 6 June 1805.
22. BL, OIOC, SSFR, G/34/23 (6 July to 28 December 1809), see the minute by Philips on 30 November 1809.
23. J. F. A. Mc Nair, assisted by W. D. Bayliss, *Prisoners Their Own Warders: A Record of the Convict Prison at Singapore: Together with a Cursory History of the Convict Establishments at Bencoolen, Penang and Malacca from the Year 1797*, London, 1899.
24. BL, OIOC, SSFR, 1805-25, G/34/23, (6 July to 28 December 1809), see the minute by Mr. Philips dated 30 November 1809.

25. BL, OIOC, *Madras Judicial Consultations*, 1805-25 (hereafter MJC), P/322/45 (1 February to 27 March 1810), see the letter of T. Raffles to A. Falconar dated 23 March 1810.
26. BL, OIOC, G/34/29.
27. BL, SSFR, 1814, G/34/43 (6 January to 30 April 1814), petitions and minute by William Petrie dated 4 February 1814 and 5 February 1814.
28. BL, MJC 1814, P/323/4 (25 February to 22 March 1814), see the letter of W. A. Clubley to G. Strachey dated 25 February 1814.
29. BL, MJC, 1814, P/323/7, see the letter of R. H. Young to government dated 25 February 1814, 22 April 1814 and 7 June 1814.
30. Anand Yang, 'Indian Convict Workers in Southeast Asia in the Late Eighteenth and Early Nineteenth Centuries', *Journal of World History*, vol. 14, no. 2, 2003, pp. 179-208.
31. BL, SSFR, 1815, G/34/49 (6 April 1815 to 12 July 1815), see petitions, 11 April 1815 and 21 April 1815.
32. BL, SSFR, 1817, G/34/62 (9 September 1817 to 27 December 1817), see the letter of D. Hill to Clubley dated 9 September and 25 September 1817.
33. BL, SSFR, 1818, G/34/56 (6 July 1818 to 7 October 1818), see the minute by Governor Bannerman dated 7 September 1818.
34. BL, SSFR, 1817, G/34/60 (2 January 1817 to 12 April 1817), see the minutes by president dated 23 January 1817.
35. James Welsh, Military Reminiscences, p. 135.
36. Ibid.
37. BL, OIOC, F/4/635 (17222 to 17316) see no. 17224, BC, India 1818, see the extract of judicial letter to Madras dated 4 March 1818.
38. BL, SSFR, G/34/72 (26 August 1819 to 23 December 1819), see the letter of Coombs to government dated 10 December 1819.
39. BL, MJC, 1820, P/323/60, (15 September 1820 to 14 November 1820) see the letter of D. Hill to police dated 27 October 1820, and police to government dated 3 November 1820.
40. BL, MJC, 1825, P/324/ 3, (11 November 11 1825 to 30 December 1825) see the letter of magistrate to government dated 27 September 1825.
41. BL, OIOC, F/4/63317169.
42. BL, OIOC, F/4/2625837, see the police regulations.
43. BL, OIOC, F/4/74020284, Census Department, 1823, Prince of Wales Island.
44. BL, OIOC, SSFR, G/34/89.
45. James Low, *The British Settlement of Penang*, Singapore, 1836.
46. Nordin Hussin, *Trade and Society in the Straits of Melaka: Dutch Melaka and English Penang, 1780-1830*, Singapore, 2009, on British administration, pp. 237-62, on Asian and European community, pp. 293-312.
47. T. J. Newbold, Political and Statistical Account, p. 44.
48. Tamil Nadu State Archives (hereafter, TNSA), Chennai, *Madras Public*

Proceedings (hereafter MPP), vol. 836, no. 7, Letter of the Governor of Prince of Wales Island to Officiating Chief Secretary at Fort St. George dated 15 May 1849.

49. Ibid., MPP, vol. 832, nos. 7–8, Letter of the Official Resident Councilor of the Prince of Wales Island to the Officiating Chief Secretary at Fort St. George dated 12 December 1848.
50. Ibid., MPP, vol. 836, no.7, Letter of the Governor of Prince of Wales Island to Officiating Chief Secretary at Fort St. George dated 15 May 1849.
51. Ibid., MPP, vol. 832, nos. 7-8, Letter of the Official Resident Councilor of Prince of Wales Island to Officiating Chief secretary at Fort St. George dated 12 December 1848.
52. TNSA, MPP, vol. 832, nos. 7–8, See the appendix, Ships Arriving in Prince of Wales Island dated 12 December 1848.
53. Archives Nationales, Section Outre-Mer (hereafter ANSOM), Paris, Inde 465, D. 595, P.V. de la séance du 10 Novembre 1855 du 10 Novembre 1855 de conseil administration.
54. Roucaia Badat, *Un Comptoir Francais des Indes: Karaikal de 1850 a 1862*, Memoire de Maitrise d' Histoire, Universite de Aix-en-Provence, 1972, p. 110.
55. Ibid., pp. 43-5.
56. Centre des Archives de Outre-Mer (hereafter CAOM), Aix-en-Provence, Karaikal 1861, Dossier 77, pp. 56v-57v (13 Novembre 1861).
57. National Archives of India (hereafter NAI), New Delhi, Department of Revenue, Agriculture and Commerce: Emigration Branch (hereafter DRACEB), Proceedings 1–9, September 1871, see Letter of J. W. Birch to the Chief Secretary at Fort St. George dated 1 July 1870.
58. BL, *Report of the Penang Riots Commission*, Penang, 1867.
59. Sunil S. Amrith, *Crossing the Bay of Bengal: The Furies of Nature and the Fortunes of Migrants*, Cambridge, Harvard University Press, 2013, pp. 101-103.
60. Ibid.
61. Hugh Tinker, *A New System of Slavery: The Export of Indian Labour Overseas, 1830-1900*, London, 1974, pp. 110-2.
62. Ibid., p. 103.
63. NAI, DRACEB, Proceedings of 1–9, September 1871, Letter of Harry St George Ord to the Earl of Kimberley dated 15 May 1871.
64. Charles Burton Buckley, *An Anecdotal History of Old Times in Singapore (With Portraits and Illustrations): From the Foundation of the Settlement under the Honourable the East India Company, on February 6th, 1819, to the Transfer of the Colonial Office as Part of the Colonial Possessions of the Crown on April 1st, 1867*, II vols., Fraser & Neave, Singapore, 1902, vol. 1, pp. 73, 83-6; C.E., Wurtzburg, *Raffles of the Eastern Isles*, Oxford University Press, Singapore, 1954, p. 69.
65. Sofia Raffles, *Memoir of the Life and Public Services of Sir Thomas Stamford Raffles*, Oxford University Press, Singapore, 1830, reprint, 1991, p. 20.

66. Lee Kam Hing, *The Sultanate of Aceh: Relations with the British 1760-1824*, Oxford University Press, Kuala Lumpur, 1995, pp. 160, 189.
67. Charles Burton Buckley, An Anecdotal History, vol. 1, p. 119.
68. Ibid., p. 154
69. Ibid., p. 85.
70. Ibid. p. 86.
71. Ibid., p. 312.
72. BL, OIOC, SSFR, G/34/153, Singapore Diary, 1827.
73. Charles Burton Buckley, An Anecdotal History, vol. 1, p. 332; 'Criminal Session', The Singapore Free Press, 3 May 1866; 'Local', The Singapore Free Press, 17 May 1866; 'Local', The Singapore Free Press, 7 June 1866.
74. Stephen Dobbs, *The Singapore River: A Social History 1819-2002*, Singapore University Press, Singapore, 2003, pp. 38-43; Charles Burton Buckley, An Anecdotal History, vol. 1, see 'Local', The Singapore Free Press, 11 October 1866.
75. Charles Burton Buckley, An Anecdotal History, vol. II, pp. 626-7.
76. Louis S. Jackson, 'Census of Singapore and Its Dependencies, Taken under Orders of Government in the Months of November and December 1849', *The Journal of the Indian Archipelago and Eastern Asia*, 4 February: Tables I & II. p. 106, see Table II.
77. Ibid., see Table II, 1850, pp. 106-7.
78. Charles Burton Buckley, An Anecdotal History, see 'Local', The Singapore Free Press, 16 August 1866.
79. Ibid., 'Local', The Singapore Free Press, 28 June 1866; 'Local', The Singapore Free Press, 16 August 1866; 'Criminal Session', The Singapore Free Press, 11 October 1866; James William Norton Kyshe, ed., *Cases Heard and Determined in Her Majesty's Supreme Court of the Straits Settlements 1808-1884*: Civil Cases, Singapore and Straits Printing Office, Singapore, 1885, vol. 1, p. 201.
80. Charles Burton Buckley, An Anecdotal History, vol. 1, p. 364.
81. Ibid., The Singapore Free Press, 8 February 1866.
82. Ibid., Supplement to the Singapore Free Press, 26 April 1866.
83. Ibid., Charles Burton Buckley, An Anecdotal History, vol. II, pp. 557-9.
84. Ibid., 'Criminal Session', The Singapore Free Press, 19 April 1866.
85. Ibid., Supplement to the Singapore Free Press, 10 May 1866.
86. National Archives of Singapore (hereafter NAS), *Straits Settlements Records: Singapore Consultations* (hereafter SSRSC), A34, May 1827, see the petition from the Hindu inhabitants of Singapore.
87. NAS, SSRSC, A34, May 1827, see the petition from the Hindu inhabitants of Singapore; see also petition from Mohammedan inhabitants of Singapore respecting the Hindu temple adjoining the mosque.
88. NAS, *Miscellaneous Letters Out, 1800–1867*, V30, 1860, see the letter to the trustees, Hindu temple at Singapore.
89. Charles Burton Buckley, An Anecdotal History, vol. II, p. 645.

90. Ibid., vol. 1, p. 375; vol. II, pp. 505, 657, 723.
91. Ibid., The Singapore Free Press, 23 November 1865; 'Criminal Session', The Singapore Free Press, 19 April 1866, 26 April 1866, 3 May 1866 & 10 May 1866; Supplement to the Singapore Free Press, 26 April 1866 and 10 May 1866.

Chapter - 7

Conclusion

The East India Companies when they set sail their ships on voyages to India in the early modern age they made labour recruitment of sailors, seamen, physicians and naval surgeons in Europe as their employees for the company service. Some workers were also hired. These trading companies also recruited soldiers, seamen, artisans, dock-workers in Tamil country and employed to meet out their local needs. Thus there developed a neat distinction of labour between those workers recruited and originated in Europe and in Tamil country.

Slaves from the Tamil coast and hinterland had moved abroad under the banner of the trading companies in the beginning stage of European commercial expansion on the coast. They were employed in building fortifications, loading and unloading ships, growing food for local consumption, hired out as artisans and apprentices, served European families as domestic servants and transient sailors in the various port settlements in Asia. There was also substantial number of free workers of Tamil country who moved overseas besides floating Tamil trading population particularly merchants and traders going around Asia in the early modern age.

Labour transfers from Tamil country came to develop typical of modern capitalist economies distinct from earlier waves of temporary or trading migrations. It happened during the expanding colonial age and the migration of Tamils had affected the coast and hinterland whose inhabitants came to be scattered around the world. Labour mobility extended in an increasing manner to Mauritius, Reunion, French West Indies, Ceylon and Malaya in different forms and at different rates. The growth in forms of employment which Tamil workers enjoyed fixed term contract engagements through work agencies/contractors. The exodus from Tamil country was both more intensive and more long-lasting than from any other part of the sub-continent. It started shortly before complete integration of the Tamil regional economy into the world-system, which dates from the introduction of export-oriented agriculture.

Tamil immigrants in large scale moved overseas mainly after 1834. An examination and analysis of primary sources shows employment trends that had a systematic and massive increase in labour flexibility not only by employing more of temporary and contract labour. There were pull and push factors. The pull was the promised opportunities. The push was the migrants' decision to indenture themselves. I have paid more attention to the role played by institutions, employers, politics and the inventiveness of Tamil migrants themselves in shaping the labour markets instead of theorization the production relations that determined migration. I have also more closely looked at the ways in which the Tamils adapted to the experience of migration.

I

The French East India Company in Pondicherry for the first time recruited only the skilled workers to Mauritius in 1729 under a contract executed for a period of three years. Later on from 1841 to 1883 the company had enacted a law that the workers should sign a contract for a minimum period of five years and the French in Pondicherry and Karaikal sent labourers in ships to Mauritius and Reunion islands. However when the workers were sent to Guadeloupe, Martinique and French Guiana they had to sign a contract for a period of three years alone. The Anglo-French convention signed in 1861 opened up the British ports to recruiters for Reunion and the French Caribbean. It legalized the export of Tamil indentured labourers to the French colonies.

The English East India Company in Madras recruited and sent labourers to Mauritius in 1829 and the workers had to sign a contract for a period of five years. In 1865 the contract period was reduced to three years and this legislation was particularly introduced because the workers were not willing and ready and available for migration. The wages of the workers per month was though fixed at five rupees in 1829, it was increased to seven rupees in 1842 and it further had been enhanced to nine rupees in 1865, labourers were not abundantly available for export from Madras.

The English in Madras made efforts to recruit workers for Ceylon in 1828 and the contract period signed was only for one year. The contract period was increased in 1844 to a period of three years. Though the Ordinance No. 5 of 1851 introduced had proposed to recruit labourers from Telugu speaking areas and remote districts of the Northern Circars of the Madras Presidency with a contract for three years, it was not implemented. Therefore a new Ordinance No. 20 of 1861 was passed, by which owners of the estates in Ceylon were enabled to enter into contracts for the hire and service of persons for any period exceeding one month but not exceeding three years. This Ordinance of 1861 was succeeded by Ordinance No. 11 of 1865 which was called the Master—Servant law of 1865 that introduced strict labour regulations in Ceylon.

The English Company in Madras exported workers to Malaya with the contract period fixed for five years. Thus according to time and place the English and the French East India Companies on the Tamil coast had introduced and executed various periods of time for the labour contract.

II

The ships from Pondicherry sailed to France normally in the months of January and February. These ships with the labourers recruited first touched Mauritius and then Reunion islands in April and May. Generally the voyage lasted around 60 days. In one instance we find the voyage had taken 44 days. Ships sailed to Guadeloupe, Martinique and French Guiana from Pondicherry took around 90 days to 126 days. A ship from Karaikal departed on 25 August 1866 arrived Guadeloupe on 12 November 1866. Again A ship from Pondicherry that departed on 21 December 1866 had arrived Guadeloupe on 6 April 1867. The voyages were very long and tedious and so the labourers also suffered because of sea sickness.

The *thonies*, boats and small ships from Pamban and Rameswaram carrying workers took five hours to reach Thalaimannar in Ceylon. Similarly the boats of Tuticorin took 20 hours to reach Ceylon. The cost of sailing from Pamban was one rupee and the cost of sailing from Tuticorin was three rupees. The English ships from Madras to Mauritius in 1829 took an average of 33 days of sail. According to the then prevailed system the ships to Mauritius left in May, June, August, September and October. The ships to Malaya sailed between July and mid-September. The English ships that sailed to Penang took 76 days. Thus the duration of sailing for the long distance voyages and the short distance voyages had varied.

III

While recruiting and exporting the workers overseas the age of the migrant was of primary concern for the companies. The French in

Pondicherry fixed the minimum age of the coolie as 16 and those below than that were not permitted. Again the coolies sailing to Martinique, Guadeloupe and French Guiana were fixed between the age of 14 and 30.

The English in Madras had fixed that those above the age of 16 and below the age of 30 to sign contracts for work in the plantations in Mauritius. The English Company had not fixed any age limit for those who sailed to work in the plantations in Ceylon. Hence many families had sailed with their kids and children. It has been found in records that in the beginning men rarely brought their wives and children and the resulting separation from normal family life provided a stimulus for a quick return to Tamil coast.

IV

The life cycle of the coolie labourers were broadly of five different stages. The first was the recruitment and travel from the hinterland village to the port of embarkation on the Tamil coast. The second was the migration and sailing voyage from the port of the Tamil coast to the port in the overseas country. The third was from the depot of the labourers in the overseas country to the plantation estate where the coolie had been destined for work. The fourth was the employment and hard labour put up at the estate toiling hard for earning wages and towards repaying the debts incurred. The fifth was the completion of the contract period and leaving for the Tamil motherland. In some cases they again had to enter into another contract in order to repay the debt.

The French East India Company officials in Pondicherry had entered into labour contracts with 87,083 coolie labourers between 1849 and 1882. Among them 25,075 persons had returned to Tamil country on expiry of the term of contract. Hence it is revealed that one worker out the four coolies who went abroad had returned to Pondicherry. But after 1861 two workers out of three coolies did not return to Pondicherry after the expiry of the terms of contract and they continued to stay in Mauritius and Reunion islands. The migration of coolie labourers from Pondicherry to Mauritius between 1851 and 1879 had been 32,000, and to Martinique islands 25,509 and to Guadeloupe 42,326. Among them 4,260 coolies on expiry of the period of contract had returned from Martinique islands between 1855 and 1882. Similarly 8,981 coolies had returned from Guadeloupe to Tamil country.

The officials of the English East India Company in Madras had recruited and sent 1,19,815 coolies from Tamil country to Mauritius between 1850 and 1890. The British government in Mauritius in 1853 promulgated an order banning the coolies for the return to Madras. Hence the coolies were put to hardships. However in 1888 an order was passed for the return of the coolies and so only a few got the chance to return to Tamil coast.

The coolies from Tamil country in large number had sailed to Ceylon. According to statistics 27,72,904 workers sailed between 1839 and 1883. Among them 21,56,460 had returned to Tamil coast on expiry of the terms of contract. Hence it is noted that 6,16,444 coolie labourers had stayed away in Ceylon. As per records, we find (during the eight years period alone) between 1862 and 1870, 1,26,064 labourers had continued to stay back in Ceylon without returning to Tamil coast. The English in Madras recruited coolies from Tamil country to Penang in Malaya and we find 18,634 workers had sailed during 1850 and 1862. Similarly 12,973 coolies had migrated to Singapore in the same period.

Under the French rule in Pondicherry there functioned the emigration society in 1851. Hence passport was issued to the coolies for migration to Mauritius. There functioned one agency in Pondicherry and another at Karaikal for the exclusive recruitment of coolies to the French West Indies. Further, private individuals also functioned as recruiting agents. In order to regulate the affairs of labour recruitment, the French company allowed and fixed a sum of three rupees more to the private parties than the company run emigration society. In the sailing voyages to the French West Indies we find that the death rate of coolies ranging from seven percent to 14 percent.

When the English in Madras recruited coolies for the sugarcane plantations in Mauritius in 1838, it is gleaned that coolies were largely from the caste of *pallars*. In 1843 the company had appointed an officer titled 'Protector of the Emigrants'. After that we notice the *vellalars*, *pariayars*, *padayatchi*, *kallars* and barber caste in large number were recruited as labourers and they had sailed away. Since 1875 we find *reddiyars*, *kaikolars*, *saliyars* and *muchiyars* had migrated in large number. The salary of six months in cash was given in advance to the labour migrants in Madras and it included the cost of shipping. Sometimes three months salary in cash was given in advance and the remaining three months salary was apportioned towards the cost of passage. The English East India Company in Madras followed a policy of gender ratio in migration and it normally consisted of 100 coolies of men and 40 coolies women in a single voyage.

The coffee planters association in Ceylon came forward to recruit labourers needed from Tamil country. It appointed a *kangaani* and he was sent to recruit the coolies and transport them in boats and small ships to

Ceylon. The ports of Rameswaram and Tuticorin came to function very brisk. Coolies were transported in government ferries and private boats from Tamil coast to Ceylon. Tamils who migrated had suffered owing to the different climatic conditions in the coffee estates. As a result many of them became sick too. Those who violated the terms of labour contract were severely punished. The working hours fixed had been from 6 in the morning to 10 in the morning and again from 12.00 in the noon to 5.30 in the evening. Labour laws were made strict and followed. Those who did not do the work properly and those who were not punctual were punished. It varied normally from three months jail to a fine of five pounds. According to records the coolies migrated to Ceylon were chiefly from the districts of Thanjavur, Madurai and Tirunelveli.

Hindu and Muslim merchants from the Tamil coast had sailed in ships to Penang in Malaya. The English East India Company sent the *paalayakarar* convicts from Tamil coast to Penang. Some of them returned after 25 years. The migration of coolies from the Tamil coast to Penang was 33,948 between 1848 and 1862. Similarly 12,973 coolies had sailed away to Singapore during 1825 and 1860. As per the terms of labour contract the coolies worked for six days in a week and ten hours per day. The cost of passage was recovered from the monthly salary of the coolies within two years.

V

The circumstances which prevailed in Tamil country in the age of expanding colonial development came to seriously affect the living conditions of the people. There prevailed failure of monsoon and agriculture, famines along with poverty. The escalation of prices and unemployment drove the people to migrate overseas to earn for their livelihood. The French and the English East India Companies took this opportunity and recruited coolie labourers through brokers and agents. The coolies recruited in bulk came from the same families and most of them were near relatives hailing from one village or the surrounding villages. Over a period of time when many *kangannis* became agents and brokers, people of many castes came to be recruited as coolies. As a result the large demand of labour for the companies came to be fulfilled.

It is known that the brahmins did not mix with other castes and so their contacts in Tamil society were very limited. Having migrated inland from other parts of India to Tamil country for centuries together they experienced the pains and sufferings of migration. Therefore they did not wish and prefer to migrate overseas. They knew that there was no opportunity for them to conduct rituals because there were no temples in the colonies. There was also no possibility of patronage to vedic studies and learning of Sanskrit in these overseas colonies. The brahmins themselves did not have any technical skill and adaptation to manual labour. Hence they had abstained from overseas migration. Further *mukkuvars*, *paravars*, *sembadavars*, *pattanavars*, *valaiyars* of the fishing communities also did not migrate overseas for there was no necessity to go for fishing or doing job in the overseas. The landlords, the rich and the wealthy men did not migrate overseas for there was no need. In 1865 we find some merchants of Nagapattinam seeking permission from the English East India Company to migrate to Mauritius and they reached Mauritius to conduct business and trade.

In the area of Thanjavur the population had steadily decreased between 1779 and 1789 owing to continuous wars. It had ranged from one million to, 6,50,000 by the end of the eighteenth century. The region of Sirkazhi and Mayavaram was depopulated highly and the areas of Kumbakonam and Mannargudi had slight depopulation as found in the records. The population in Chingleput district decreased in the beginning of the nineteenth century. In Madras district the population had kept on going down continuously. In the regions of North Arcot, South Arcot, Tiruchirapalli, Madurai and Tirunelveli the population had well decreased in the first half of the nineteenth century. The main reason for the decrease in population in Tamil country was that the families and people in large number had left their villages and sought employment overseas and they had migrated.

VI

There developed high labour demand with the dawn of British colonial rule around the world in the nineteenth century. People from various parts of India had migrated overseas but we are only concerned with Tamil labour migration. When the English East India Company rule ended in India in 1857 and thereafter when the Crown rule was introduced we find new policies of imperial in nature came to be adopted. Mass migration of Tamil labourers had developed after 1870 to the coffee plantations in Ceylon, sugarcane plantations in Natal, South Africa, to the rubber estates of Perak in Malaya and for the rice cultivation in Burma too. It must be said that vast quantities of labour power had to be consumed at that time. The British needed plenty of workers to clear land, to bring it into conditions suitable for planting, vast acreages had to be planted, tended and ultimately harvested. In a way it was almost impossible to recruit workers without the employment of coercive or deceptive techniques. Neither free labour nor local labour in the colonies could readily enter these industries given the nature of the work, rewards and discipline. Neither slaves nor free wage labour was then available. The only solution seemed to be long-distance recruitment from Tamil country using the indenture system. Those migrated in this peak period of colonial development had to fight against their human rights when denied to them. The policy of racism followed and the absence of labour unions led to miserable condition of the workers. The study of migration of the Tamils between 1875 and 1947 had to be viewed and situated independently and differently. The multiple faces of Tamil labour migration under the imperial rule show that that the British and the French colonial administration in Tamil country at that time came to function in the interests of the employers rather than to protect workers. The administration in the overseas colonies had acted on the planters' behalf by reducing wages and lengthening indenture contracts. The colonial authorities and planters had colluded to draw a cloak of secrecy over actual conditions on the estates. The legislation introduced to improve the workers' conditions was often ineffective. Commissions investigating worker abuse rarely made recommendations detrimental to planters. The Protectors of Immigrants were often friends of the planters and shared their class background and interests. Further, the tie between the Tamil migrant labourer and *kangaani* was a major cause of exploitation.

At first it must be said that migration was not an individual action. It was an organized system whereby the colonialist had the lead and control. It was not that the labourers were offering themselves for work on the plantations. Secondly the system of recruitment was based on deception. The workers agreed to a contract without any idea of what they were going to experience in a system of oppression and exploitation. The reality of indentured labour was hidden in the recruitment. The distress of peasants and agricultural workers was accentuated by the numerous experiments in land tenure in Tamil country initiated by the English East India Company after the middle of the eighteenth century.

Three schools of thought had emerged while dealing with overseas labour migration and diaspora studies. According to some labour overseas under indenture system as a new system of slavery. The image of the migrant was said as a victim of various forms of greed, deception and colonial coercion/manipulation. It has been said that unfreedom was the distinguishing character of indenture, whereby the worker was unable to withdraw/discontinue his or her labour power to bargain/negotiate over the terms of contract for better wages and living conditions. Secondly the scholars of coercion point of view had stressed the ignorance of the labourers and argue that they were misled and misinformed by recruiters regarding the nature of plantation work and were even made captives and transported overseas against their free will. Hence, in such cases it is not possible to define migration as a free choice. The workers were often drawn into debt trap/bondage by the labour recruiters and the contractual relations between the employers and the employees were not really voluntary. It has also been emphasized that the employers used extra-economic and penal methods to control labour and the workers were forced to live in a state of virtual bondage. Thirdly, the imperialist, colonialist and revisionist school suggests that migration was made economically beneficial. It has been suggested by revisionists that long distance migration movements of indentured labour has clearly revealed that the considerable improvements achieved over time in living and working conditions made this migration stream a small but important escape hatch for migrant labourers from motherland. Further, it argues that indentured emigration to overseas colonies was the result of rational and deliberate choice on the part of migrants, prompted by hopes of bettering their future. The central flaw of the theories is their failure to analyze crucial changes in recruiting strategies which helped to maintain the dynamism of overseas labour mobilization.

In my opinion all these approaches tend to view the emigrant either as an object of sympathy or appreciation, and neglected to take into account the subjective considerations involved in the migration process and its complex patterns. These scholars had either put forth emphasis on subsistence-oriented push factors or betterment-oriented pull factors as the most important determinant of emigration. The proponents of new slavery theory, for instance, have ignored the fact that over a period of time migrant labourers were increasingly familiarized with the conditions abroad through relatives, friends and neighbours and that the choice of a destination by a prospective migrant also depended on migration patterns and strategies comprising networks of kith, kin and family as well as fellow-villagers and friends, who often provided vital information. My research here clearly shows that the debates about whether or not the emigrants were free or unfree ignored the complex and multi-dimensional historical reality and reduced the whole migration process into its most simple form of either this or that. What has been forgotten is the fact that migration of labour under colonial/imperial conditions was varied and mixed. No unilinear pattern of transition from free to unfree labour could be discerned in the case of Tamil migrations. It can also be said that free and unfree types of migration were also socially conditioned. In the case of Tamil coast, the vast majority of lower castes were subjected to debt-bondage and hence their migration was forced and involuntary, i.e., the migrant labourers were more pushed than pulled. Therefore migration is conceptualized as unity and continuous process, although the motives and aspirations of individual migrants and social groups differed substantially. The massive labour emigration since 1875 had only marked great movement in the historical context which ultimately had led to the planting of Tamil communities far beyond the borders of their motherland.

Bibliography

I: MANUSCRIPTS

France

1. Archives Nationales, Section Outre-Mer, Paris

Serie Geographique

Inde 464

Dossier 590, Letter of the Governor of Pondicherry to the Ministry of Marine dated 1 December 1849

Dossier 590, Letter of Governor Bedier to Ministry dated 23 May 1851

Inde 465

Dossier 594, Letter of Minister to de Verninac dated 23 April 1853

Dossier 595, Letter of Verninac to Minister dated 18 July 1855

Dossier 595, P.V. de la séance du 10 Novembre 1855 du 10 Novembre 1855 de conseil administration

Dossier 599, Ministerial dispatch of 23 January 1857

Inde 466

Dossier 600, P.V. de la séance du 16 Octobre 1858 du conseil administration

Dossier 600, Etat indiquant le nombre emigrants expedies aux Antilles du 1er Janvier 1858 au 21 Octobre suivant

Dossier 600, Letter no. 380, of August 1859, d'Ubraye to Ministre

Dossier 600, Lettre du Gouverneur d'Ubraye au Minister du 26 Juillet 1859, no. 328; Etat recapitulatif des emigrants de tous age, embarque de Pondichery et de Karikal sur les navires de la compagnie generale maritime du 1er Janvier au 28 Octobre 1859

Dossier 600, Etat Recapitulatif des engages embarques des Repenses, des recettes et des benefices faits par la Societe d' Emigration suivant ses livres du 27 Juin 1859 au 23 Mai 1861

Dossier 600, letter of Ubraye of 10 Octobre 1860 of no. 497 and 23 Novembre 1860 of no. 502

Inde 467

Dossier 607, Releve des batiments qui ont transporte des Indiens dans nos colonies d' Amerique avant et depuis la convention, avec indication des mortalities survenues durant la traverse

Dossier 607, Tableau des immigrants Indieas introduits a la Martinique a la Guadeloupe et a la Guyane pendant les annees 1864 et 1846

Inde 468

Dossier 608, Etat des emigrants de L'Inde depuis le 1er Janvier 1866

Carton de la Reunion, 454

Dossier 5052, Tableau construit avec les statistiques des dossiers, Annee 1861

Dossier 5053, Tableau construit avec les statistiques des dossiers, Annee 1862

Dossier 5054, Tableau construit avec les statistiques dos dossiers, Annee 1863

Dossier 5055, Tableau construit avec les statistiques des dossiers, Annee 1864

Dossier, 5056, Tableau construit avec les statistiques dos dossiers, Annee 1865

Dossier 5057, Tableau construit avec les statistiques des dossiers, Annee 1866

Dossier 5058, Tableau construit avec les statistiques dos dossiers, Annee 1867

Dossier 5059, Tableau construit avec les statistiques des dossiers, Annee 1868

Dossier, 5060, Tableau construit avec les statistiques dos dossiers, Annee 1869

Dossier 5061, Tableau construit avec les statistiques des dossiers, Annee 1870

Dossier 5062, Tableau construit avec les statistiques des dossiers, Annee 1871

Dossier 5063, Tableau construit avec les statistiques des dossiers, Annee 1872

Dossier 5064, Tableau construit avec les statistiques des dossiers, Annee 1873

Dossier 5072, Tableau construit avec les statistiques des dossiers, Annee 1882

Dossier 5073, Tableau construit avec les statistiques des dossiers, Annee 1883

Dossier 5074, Etat des immigrants nes Repatries et morts a la Reunion depuis 1848 et jusqu' en 1866, fait a Paris le 21 Mai 1867 pour les annee posterieures a 1866, ont et e utilisees les statistiques des dossiers Reunion

2. Centre des Archives de Outre-Mer, Aix-en Provence

Série FM

SG/Reu c 406, c 432 d 4603 a‘ 4606

SG/Inde 464, d. 590

Guadeloupe 1866

Chemise 183, Dossier 1126.

Guyane 1819

Extraite d' une letter ecrite de Fr Louis Senegel en date du 12 Avril 1819 a son excellence, la Ministre de la Marine, par M. Mahe, capitaine de vaisseau, introduction d' Indiens a la Guiane francaise, 1818-1822.

Guyane 1862

Process–verbaux de la Commission instiutee par decisison du Gouverneur en date du 28 Janvier 1862, a l'effet de proceder a une enquete sur l'etat moral et sanitaire des immigrants indiens introduite dans la colonie par le navire Le Parmentier' Convoi du Parmentier, partie de Pondichery 25 Mars 1861 arrive a Cayenne 9 Juillet 1861.

Inde 1863

Envoie du catalogue des ouvrages en langue tamoule edites par l'Imprimerie de la mission, Letter from the Governor to Minister of the Marine and Colonies, written from Pondichery dated 18 February 1863, Circulire addressee aux colonies et relative a une souscription a des ouvrages en langue tamoule edites par l'Imprimerie de la mission Catholique en Inde, 1863-1865.

Karaikal, 1861

Dossier 77

INDIA

3. National Archives of India, New Delhi

Department of Revenue, Agriculture and Commerce:Emigration Branch

Proceedings 1–9, September 1871, Letter of J. W. Birch to the Chief Secretary at Fort St. George dated 1 July 1870

Proceedings of 1–9, September 1871, Letter of Harry St George Ord to the Earl of Kimberley dated 15 May 1871

4. Tamilnadu State Archives, Chennai

Accounts and Papers

vol 25: Correspondence by the Government of India dated 18 September 1838

Madras Public Proceedings

vol. 832, nos. 7–8, Letter of the Official Resident Councilor of the Prince of Wales Island to the Officiating Chief Secretary at Fort St. George dated 12 December 1848

vol. 832, nos. 7–8, The Ships Arriving in Prince of Wales Island dated 12 December 1848

vol. 836, no. 7, Letter of the Governor of Prince of Wales Island to Officiating Chief Secretary at Fort St. George dated 15 May 1849

MALAYSIA

5. Arkib Negara Malaysia, Kuala Lumpur

Microfilm of Straits Settlements Factory Records, vol. 6 (1794) to vol. 13 (1806)

MAURITIUS

6. National Archives of Mauritius

Série A

A. 41, Register pour server a l'enregisterement des actes d'affranchissement accordes aux esclaves de Port-Louis, Municipalite de Port-Louis, 1796-1800

A. 143, no.276, Land deen Notary Macquet, 25 Octobre 1856, Reg. C88, No.1650, March 1863

Série E

17B, Comite de surete publique, Register des cautionnements 1793-1803

Série G

GA 2, Gouvernment Imperial

Série J

JL 24, Conseilde famille, 7 Floreal An Onze

Série K

KK3, Census of 1804

Série N

NA, 38/12 c , 22 fevrier 1806-11-Avril 1807, Minutes de notaire, J.F. Arnaud

NA 50/10 B, Inventaire après le deces de Maria Saron, veuve Chavriage An 9 Minutes de notaire L.D. Durand,

Série O

OA/85, Bureau de Police, 7 Juin 1784

OA/ 85, Bureau de Police, Jurisdiction Royale, 12 Avril 1785

OA/ 85, Bureau de Police, 9 Decembre 1786

OA/ 85, Bureau de Police (Instruction Royale), Livre pour server a L'enregisterment de divers orders, letters et autres pieces ayant trait aux functions de police, 22 Novembre 1799- 14 Avril 1787

PA Series: *Immigration-letters rceived: Letters received by the Protector of Immigrants from other Government Departments*

PA 12, District Magistrate of Grand Port, Report no. 206 of 1871

PA 14, Letter of M. Perot to M. Aubin dated 10 October 1872

PA 14, Letter of Inspector of Government Reformatory to Beyts dated 26 January 1872

PA 43, Petition of Vencatachellum Appoo dated 23 August 1880; Immigration Department Report dated 1 September 1880

PA 48, Letter of the Stipendiary Magistrate of Flacq to the Protector of Immigrants dated 4 June 1881

PA 57, Letter of the Emigration Agent to the Secretary of the Government of Madras dated 24 February 1843

PA 60, Letter of Allamalloo to Protector of Immigrants dated 8 March 1884; Immigration Office Note dated 12 March 1884

PA 68, Poor Law Commissioner to Protector of Immigrants, Protector's Note dated 28 April 1885; Immigration Office Note dated 29 April 1885

PA 111, Petition of Immigrant Lotah submitted on his behalf by the clerk of Constance Sugar Estate to the Protector of Immigrants on 22 June 1889

PA 204, Immigration Department Minutes, dated 14 September 1899

PA 206, Letter of Ameenee to Protector of Immigrants dated 19 October 1899

PB Series: *Immigration letters sent: Letters of the Protector of Immigrants to other Government Departments*

PB 5, Protector's Report, 13 November 1855

PL Series: *Letters and Petitions*

PL 79, Petition of Nagen and Camatchee dated 8 September 1868

RA Series: *General Correspondence: Letters received 1834-74: Information concerning immigration department*

RA 416, Letter of Finiss to Barry dated 26 October 1829

RA 417, letter of Finiss to Barry dated 27 November 1829

RA 418, Letter of Finiss to Barry dated 17 December 1829

RA 552, Letter of Charles Anderson, Special Magistrate of Port Louis to Mr. Hardy of Argy Sugar Estate dated 30 August 1836

RA 1081, Letter of the Emigration agent of Madras to Colonial Secretary dated 2 September 1850

RA 1081, Contract between Henry Wood Gabb the Emigration Agent and the Contractor P.A. Pillay in March 1850

RA 1788, Report of Travelling Inspector, southern districts, 1865, Reports of Marsh and Marley

RA 1804, Letter of the Stipendiary Magistrate of Flacq to the Protector of Immigrants dated 21 February 1865

RC Series: *Petitions, 1834-44*: *Petitions Relative to Indian Immigration*

RC 25, Petition of Immigrant Lotah, Ex-Indenture Labourer from Madras, India to Acting Governor Staveley which was drafted on his behalf by the clerk of Argy Sugar Estate upon the instructions of Mr. Hardy in Flacq dated 5 June 1840

RC 26, Letter of Hardy to Anderson dated 5 September 1836

RC 34, Report of Thomy Hugon on Indian Immigration to Governor Sir William Nicolay dated 15 July 1839

Z Series

Z/2B, no. 20, Jurisdiction Royale, Register des audiences de police tenues par le Juge Royal, 22 Decembre 1773-25 Mars, 1780

7. Mahatma Gandhi Institute, Moka

PE Series : *Immigrants list of arrivals,1826-1927*

Ship Arrivals and Distribution List of Indentured Labourers for 1826 to 1842

PE Series: *Indian Immigration Registers, 1843-1873*

Ship Clarissa from Madras: Nominal list of immigrants consisting of 143 men 16 women and 3 children landed on the 8th of August 1843

Ship Apolline from Madras: Nominal list of immigrants consisting of 207 men 36 women and 14 children landed on the 24th of November 1843

Ship John Line from Madras: Nominal list of immigrants consisting of 168 men 35 women and 26 children landed on the 31st of March 1852

Ship Mary Harrison from Madras: Nominal list of immigrants consisting of 211 men 63 women and 38 children landed on the 18th of June 1853

Ship Futtay Sultan from Madras: Nominal list of immigrants consisting of 139 men 16 women and 22 children landed on the 28th of June 1853

Ship Devonshire from Madras: Nominal list of immigrants consisting of 169 men 30 women and 14 children landed on the 8th of August 1853

Ship Elizabeth from Madras: Nominal list of immigrants consisting of 142 men 58 women and 27 children landed on the 27th of May 1856

Ship Cressy Madras: Nominal list of immigrants consisting of 221 men 99 women and 16 children landed on the 27th June 1856

Ship Sea Nymph from Madras: Nominal list of immigrants consisting of 170 men 48 women and 27 children landed on the 16th of August 1857

Ship Thracian from Madras: Nominal list of immigrants consisting of 116 men 75 women and 42 children landed on the 25th of June 1860

Ship Mermaid from Madras: Nominal list of immigrants consisting of 155 men 87 women and 29 children landed on the 1st of November 1860

Ship Chatham from Madras: Nominal list of immigrants consisting of 147 men 57 women and 75 children landed on the 4th of June 1863

Ship Fair Line from Madras: Nominal list of immigrants consisting of 113 men 60 women and 68 children landed on the 27th of October 1863

Ship Mars from Madras: Nominal list of immigrants consisting of 207 men 89 women and 72 children landed on the 28th of September 1864

Ship Latona from Madras: Nominal list of immigrants consisting of 173 men 73 women and 59 children landed on the 11th of July 1872

Ship Huderee from Madras: Nominal list of immigrants consisting of 163 men 61 women and 44 children landed on the 2nd of September 1873

PF Series: *Register of Engagements entered into by Immigrants and Others*

PF 1, Register of Engagements entered into by Immigrants and Others between 1836 and 1842

PF 44, Register of Engagements entered into by Immigrants and Others, 1885

PG Series: *Ticket registers , 1870-1922: Immigrant Photo Registers*

PG 32, Immigrant Photo Register for 1886

Immigrant No. 3158, Photograph of Lotah at the Immigration Depot

PH Series: *Vagrant Register with Vagrant Pictures*

PH, 2, Vagrant Register for the period between 1870 and 1889

PI Series: *Register of Passes issued to Immigrants reported by the Police to have lost their tickets*

PI, 4, Register of Passes issued to Immigrants reported by the Police and to have lost their Tickets between1882 and 1906

PJ Series*: Immigration Department Correspodence: List of Returning Immigrants, 1857-1932*

PJ 41, Register of Indenture Ship Departures for 1880 to 1910

PO Series*: Vagrancy, Desertion and Illegal Absence Registers*

PO 10, vol. B, Warrants issued against Indian Immigrants for Vagrancy for the period between 1855 and 1878

LA REUNION

8. Archives de la Réunion, Saint-Denis

U 339, U 349

SINGAPORE

9. National Archives of Singapore

Straits Settlements Records: Singapore Consultations

A34, May 1827, The petition from the Hindu inhabitants of Singapore

A34, May 1827, The petition from the Mohammedan inhabitants of Singapore respecting the Hindu temple adjoining the mosque

Miscellaneous Letters Out, 1800–1867,

V30, 1860, The letter to the trustees, Hindu temple at Singapore

SRILANKA

10. National Archives of Sri Lanka, Colombo

Lot 41/163, No. 47 of 24 April 1856

Lot 41/163, No. 128 of 1 July 1856

UNITED KINGDOM

11. British Library, London

Oriental and India Office Collection

F/4/142, 2489, Wellesley to Clive dated 17 August 1802

F/4/262, 5837, The police regulations

F/4/740, 20284, Census Department, 1823, Prince of Wales Island

F/4/635 (17222 to 17316) The judicial letter to Madras dated 4 March 1818

F/4/919, 25850, Letter of C.M. Lushington to A.D. Campbell dated 1 July 1819

F/4/919, 25850, Letter of J. Vaughan to the Board of Revenue dated 20 July 1819

F/4/1034, 28499, Slavery, Kidnapping and Sale of children in Tanjore and Tinnevelly, 1825

F/4/1414, 55774, Relative to the Kidnapping of Children from the Company's Territory for Sale as Slaves, 1830–33

P/241/31, Letter of Mathew Yeats to Sir Charles Oakley dated 22 December 1792

P/241/36, Letter of Mathew Yeats to Major-General William Meadows dated 3 February 1792

P/252/76, Letter of Charles Oakley to Jacob Eilbracht dated 14 February 1792

Board's Collection

1803-04, F/4/155, no.2737, The letter of Rochead to government dated 8 March 1803-04

1803-04, F/4/155, no. 2737, The letter of Rochead, Fort St. George

1803-04, F/4/155, no. 2737, The letter of Leith to government

Factory Records: Straits Settlements, 1790-1827

G/34/4, Minutes and resolution of the Boards of Trade on Captain Light's letter, at Fort William, dated 14 January 1790

G/34/23, (6 July to 28 December 1809), The minutes by Mr. Philips dated 30 November 1809

G/34/43 (6 January to 30 April 1814), petitions and minute by William Petrie dated 4 February 1814 and 5 February 1814

G/34/49 (6 April 1815 to 12 July 1815), Petitions, 11 April 1815 and 21 April 1815

G/34/60 (2 January 1817 to 12 April 1817), The minutes by president dated 23 January 1817

G/34/62 (9 September 1817 to 27 December 1817), Letter of D. Hill to Clubley dated 9 September and 25 September 1817

G/34/56 (6 July 1818 to 7 October 1818), The minutes by Governor Bannerman dated 7 September 1818

G/34/153, Singapore Diary, 1827

Madras Judicial Consultations, 1810-25

P/322/45 (1 February to 27 March 1810), Letter of T. Raffles to A. Falconar dated 23 March 1810

P/323/4 (25 February to 22 March 1814), Letter of W. A. Clubley to G. Strachey dated 25 February 1814

P/323/7, Letter of R. H. Young to government dated 25 February 1814, 22 April 1814 and 7 June 1814

P/323/60, (15 September 1820 to 14 November 1820) Letter of D. Hill to police dated 27 October 1820, and police to government dated 3 November 1820

P/324/3, (11 November 11 1825 to 30 December 1825) Letter of magistrate to government dated 27 September 1825

Madras Public Proceedings, 1842-43

247/63, Finniss to Colonial Secretary, 18 June 1841

248/8, Statement of Saivaroodian, Madras Police Office, 1842

248/8, Letter of Emigration Agent to Secretary to Government, Madras, dated 21 September 1843

12. National Archives of the United Kingdom, Kew

Ceylon Blue Books

1839-1842; 1843-1849; 1850-1861

Colonial Office Records

54/227, The letter of Campbell to Earl Grey dated 11 November 1846

54/235, Letter of Tennent to Earl Grey, 21 March 1847

54/235, Letter of Emerson Tennent the Governor of Ceylon's Despatch Miscelleaneous no. 6 of 21 April 1847 to the Secretary of State for Colonies

54/235, The letter of Tennent to Earl Grey dated 21 April 1847

54/238, The Confidential letter of Torrington to Grey dated 16 August 1847

54/243, Letter of Torrington to Earl Grey dated 25 February 1847

54/299, The letter of Anderson dated 20 May 1853

54/425, No.57, Robinson to Earl of Carnaron, 6 March 1867, The minute by Roger dated 22 May 1867

54/476, No. 69 of 7 June 1872, The private letter of Gregory to Herbert dated 10 June 1872

54/477, No. 59, letter of Gregory to Earl of Kimberley dated 9 July 1872

54/492, No. 7, letter of Gregory to Earl of Kimberley dated 8 January 1874

56/2, Ceylon Acts 1841–1843

56/9, Ceylon Acts 1864–1869

UNITED STATES OF AMERICA

13. Cleveland Public Library, Ohio

MS East India Company, 1807, Report on the Origin, Progress and Termination of the Poligar Wars in the Southern Provinces

II: Printed Sources

IN FRENCH

Bonaporte, Louis-Napoléon, *Analyse de la Question des Sucres*, Administration de Librairie, Paris, 1842.

Bulletin Officiel de L'Ile Bourbon, Arrete du 10 Novembre 1843.

Bulletin Officiel de L'Ile de la Reunion, 13 February 1852.

Challaye, M.G. A de., 'Memoire sur L'immigration des Indiens et sur le travail libre dans le colonies de Maurice et de Bourbon', *Revue Coloniale*, Tome III, 1ere serie, May-August 1844, pp. 557-609.

'Emigration des coolies aux Mascareignes', *Revue Coloniale*, Mars 1845, pp. 276-98.

'Immigration des coolies aux reunion', *Revue Coloniale*, 6 Decembre 1845, p. 436.

'Immigration des coolies aux reunion', *Revue Coloniale*, Septembre-Decembre 1849, p. 320.

Le Mauricien, 15 February 1839.

Le Moniteur de la Reunion, 3 July 1852.

Rapport de M.J. Beaujean sur le voyage de Richelieu transportant un convoy d' immigrants de Pondichery a la Martinique, *Revue Coloniale*, vol. III, 1860, p. 662.

Rapport de M.A. Gaigneron sur le voyage suger transpotant un convoy d'immigrants de Pondichery a la Guadelopue, *Revue Coloniale*, vol. V, 1862, p. 712.

Schoelcher, Victor, *Polemique Coloniale, 1882-1885*: *Suivi de Discourse et Articles Divers Fort-de-France*, II vols., Paris, 1979.

IN ENGLISH

A Collection of the Laws of Mauritius and its Dependencies, 2 February 1852 to 31 December 1853, 1867, vol. VI.

A Collection of the Laws of Mauritius and its Dependencies, 1868, vol. VII.

British Parliamentary Papers: Annual Series, XXXV, 1844; Annual series, XLVII (314).

Brown, Alexander, *The Coffee Planter's Manual*, Ceylon Observer Press, Colombo, 1872.

Brown, Sampson, *Life in the Jungle*, Colombo, 1845.

Buckley, Charles Burton, *An Anecdotal History of Old Times in Singapore (With Portraits and Illustrations): From the Foundation of the Settlement under the Honourable the East India Company, on February 6th, 1819, to the Transfer of the Colonial Office as Part of the Colonial Possessions of the Crown on April 1st, 1867*, II vols., Fraser & Neave, Singapore, 1902.

Ceylon Observer, 12 March 1869, A. Joseph, 'A Tamil's account of the coffee districts of Ceylon'.

Ceylon Observer, 13 March 1869, A. Joseph,' A Tamil's account of the coffee districts of Ceylon'.

Colombo Observer, 15 June 1857, 'Letter of P. Canacaseppa reporting on the North Road dated 30 May 1857'.

Crawford, John, *History of the Indian Archipelago: Containing an Account of the Manners, Arts, Languages, Religions, Institutions and Commerce of Its Inhabitants*, 3 vols., Edinburgh, 1820.

Ferguson, A.M., *The Ceylon Districts for 1866-68*, Colombo, 1868.

Geoghegan, J., *Report on the Coolie Emigration from India*, Calcutta, 1874.

Joseph, Abraham, *Kopikrishi Kummi*, Colombo, 1869.

__________, *The Planters' Colloquial Tamil Guide and Roman Characters Or the Art of Speaking, Reading and Writing Tamil without a Teacher,* Colombo, 1872.

Kyshe, James William Norton, ed., *Cases Heard and Determined in Her Majesty's Supreme Court of the Straits Settlements 1808-1884*: Civil Cases, Singapore and Straits Printing Office, Singapore, 1885.

Leith, George, *A Short Account of the Settlement, Produce and Commerce of Prince of Wales Island in the Straits of Malacca*, London, J. Booth, 1805.

Low, James, *The British Settlement of Penang*, Singapore, 1826, reprinted OUP, Kuala Lumpur, 1972.

Maclean, C.D., *Manual of the Madras Presidency*, The Government Press, Madras, 1885.

Mc Nair, J. F. A., assisted by W. D. Bayliss, *Prisoners Their Own Warders: A Record of the Convict Prison at Singapore: Together with a Cursory History of the Convict Establishments at Bencoolen, Penang and Malacca from the Year 1797*, London, 1899.

Newbold, T.J., *Political and Statistical Account of the British Settlements in the Straits of Malacca*, 2 vols., London, 1839.

Raffles, Sofia, *Memoir of the Life and Public Services of Sir Thomas Stamford Raffles*, Oxford University Press, Singapore, 1830, reprint, 1991.

Report from Commissioners: Emigration Commission, Factories, Mines and Public Health, vol. XXII, 1862.

Report on Accounts and Paper: House of Commons for Colonies: Immigration vol. XVI.

Report on the Moral and Material Progress and Conditions of India, 1860-61, to 1889-90.

The Coffee Planter of Ceylon, second edition, Colombo, 1870.

Welsh, James, *Military Reminiscences: Extracted from a Journal of Nearly Forty Years' Active Service in the East Indies*, London, Smith, Elder, 1830.

III. Travelogues

Backhouse, James., *A Narrative of a Visit to the Mauritius and South Africa*, London: Hamilton, Adams, and Co, 1844.

Lewis, F., *Sixty-Four Years in Ceylon: Reminiscences of Life and Adventure*, Colombo, 1926.

Milbert, J.G., *Voyage Pictoresque a L'Ile de France, au Cap de Bonne Esperance et a L'Ile de Teneriffe*, II vols., Paris, 1812.

Unienville, Baron d'., *Statistique de L'Ile Maurice et ses Dependences*, Paris, tome I, 1838.

IV: Epigraphical Sources

Aiyar., K.R. Srinivasa, *Inscriptions in the Pudukottai State*, 2 Parts, Pudukottai, 1941-46.

Annual Report on Epigraphy including Indian and South Indian Epigraphy, 1881–1922, 1923–45, 1950–90, New Delhi.

Epigraphia Indica, (Govt. Pub.) Calcutta/ New Delhi (hereafter EI), 36 vols., 1892-1989.

Epigraphia Carnatica, 26 vols., Bangalore, 1886-1955.

Krishnan, K.G., *Karandhai Tamil Sangam Plates of Rajendra Cola I*, Memoirs of Archaeological Society of India, no. 79, Delhi, 1984.

Sastry., S. Subrahmanya, ed., *Tirumalai-Tirupati Devasthanam Epigraphical Series*, Madras 1931.

South Indian Inscriptions (hereafter *SII*), Publications of the Archaeological Survey of India, vols. I–XXVI, New Delhi, 1890–1990.

Srinivasan P.R., and Marie Louis Reiniche, *Tiruvannamalai, A Saiva Sacred Complex of South India, Inscriptions*, vol.1.1 and 1.2, Pondicherry, 1990.

Subramanian, T.N., *Pallavar Seppedugal Muppathu*, Madras, 1967.

Rangachari, V., *The Inscriptions of the Madras Presidency*, III vols, Madras, 1919.

Rao., T.A. Gopinatha, ed., *Travancore Archaeological Series*, Madras, 1910-13.

V. Secondary Sources

Ambirajan 'Malthusian Population Theory and Indian Famine Policy in the Nineteenth Century', *Population Studies*, vol. 30, March 1976, pp. 6-7.

Amrith, Sunil S., *The Furies of Nature and the Fortunes of Migrants*, Cambridge, Harvard University Press, 2013.

Badat, Roucaya., *Un Comptoir français des Indes: Karaikal de 1850 a 1862*, Memoire de maitrise, Universite de Aix-en-Provence, 1972.

Banerji, D.R., *Slavery in British India*, Second edition, 1933.

Barnabas, C., *From Madras to Mauritius, 1800-1856, Studies in Emigration and Assimilation*, Ph. D. Dissertation, University of Madras, 1991.

Brahy, Anne-Marie., *L'Etude des Coolies trade pour les Mascareignes de 1830 a 1865*, Memoire de maitrise, Aix-en-Provence, 1972.

Carter, Marina., *Servants, Sirdars and Settlers: Indians in Mauritius, 1834-1874*, New Delhi, OUP, 1995.

__________, *Veils from Indenture: Experiences of Indian Migrants in the British Empire*, Leicester University Press, London, 1996.

Curtin, D. Philip., *The Atlantic Slave Trade: A Census*, University of Wisconsin Press, Madison, 1969.

Daniel, E. Valentine., 'Violent Measures in the Discursive Practices of Sri Lanka's Estate Tamils', *Comparative Studies in Society and History*, vol. 35, no. 3, July 1993, pp. 568-600.

Das, N. Sonia., *Linguistic Rivalries: Tamil Migrants and Anglo-French Conflicts*, Oxford, 2016.

Dobbs, Stephen., *The Singapore River: A Social History 1819-2002*, Singapore University Press, Singapore, 2003.

Gerbeau, Hubert., 'Engagees and Coolies on Reunion Island: Slavery's Masks and Freedom's Constraints', in P.C. Emmer ed., *Colonialism and Migration: Indentured Labour before and after Slavery*, Dordrecht, 1986, pp. 210-211.

Gurukkal, Rajan., 'Non-Brahmana Resistance to the Expansion of Brahmadeyas: The Early Pandya Experience', *Proceedings of the Indian History Congress*, 45th session, Annamalai University, Chidambaram, 1984, pp. 161-63.

Hussin, Nordin., *Trade and Society in the Straits of Melaka: Dutch Melaka and English Penang, 1780-1830*, Singapore, 2009.

Jackson, Louis S., 'Census of Singapore and Its Dependencies, Taken under Orders of Government in the Months of November and December 1849', *The Journal of the Indian Archipelago and Eastern Asia*, 4 February: Tables I & II. pp. 100-106.

Jayaraman, R., 'Indian Emigration to Ceylon: Some Aspects of the Historical and Social Background of the Emigrants', *Indian Economic and Social History Review*, vol. 4, no. 4, December, 1967, pp. 319-59.

Karashima, Noboru., *South Indian History and Society: Studies from Inscriptions, AD 850-1800*, Delhi, 1984.

Krishnan, A., *Kalvettil Vaazhviyal*, Chennai, 1991.

Kumar, Dharma.,, *Land and Caste: Agricultural Labour in the Madras Presidency during the 19th Century,* Delhi, 1992.

Lalitha, V., 'Emigration of British Subjects from French Ports in India to French Colonies-Proposal to Legalise – Papers Relating to Down to 1858', *Revue Historique de Pondichery*, no. XIII, 1976 - 80, pp. 162-168.

Mazard, M. J., *L'Immigration Indienne vers les colonies françaises, 1860-1880*, Memoire de Maitrise, Aix-en-Provence, 1972.

Northrup, David., *Indentured Labor in the Age of Imperialism, 1834-1922*, Cambridge, 1995.

Peebles, P., *The Plantation Tamils of Ceylon: New Historical Perspectives on Migration*, London, 2001.

Peerthum, Satyendra., Reconsidering Crime in Port Louis: African apprentices and Indian Labourers' in A. Boraine, et al. eds., *The Report of the Truth and Justice Commission: Volume 4: History, Economy, Society and Memory: Part VIII: Indentured Immigration.* Port Louis, 2011, pp. 190-198.

Pineo, Hugette Ly Tio-Fane., *Lured Away: The Life History of Cane Workers in Mauritius*, 2nd ed. Moka, 2009.

Rajavelu, S., 'Migration of the Brahmins to Tamilandu under the Pallavas', in S. Rajagopal, ed., *Kaveri: Studies in Epigraphy, Archaeology and History*, Chennai, 2001, pp. 397-407.

Ramasamy, Vijaya., 'Traditional Crafts, Technology and Society in Pre-colonial Peninsular India', in Rajat Datta, ed., *Rethinking a Millennium: Perspectives on Indian History from the Eighth to the Eighteenth Century: Essays for Harbans Mukhia*, Delhi, 2008, pp. 275-299.

__________, 'Migrations of the Weaver Communities in Medieval Peninsular India: Thirteenth to the Eighteenth Centuries', in Vijaya Ramasamy, ed. *Migrations in Medieval and Early Colonial India*, London, 2016, pp. 165-192.

Rao, Hari., ed. *Koil Olugu*, Madras, Rochouse and Sons Pvt. Ltd, 1961.

Ratnam, R., *Agricultural Development in Madras State Prior to 1900*, Madras, 1966.

Roberts, M., 'The Master–Servant Laws of 1841 and the 1860s and Immigrant Labour in Ceylon', *Ceylon Journal of Historical and Social Studies*, vol. 8, nos. 1-2, 1965, pp. 24-37.

__________, 'Indian Estate Labour in Ceylon During the Coffee Period, 1830–1880, Part 1', *Indian Economic and Social History Review*, vol. 3, no. 1, 1966, pp. 1–52.

__________, 'Indian Estate Labour in Ceylon during the Coffee Period, 1830-1880, Part 2', *Indian Economic and Social History Review*, vol. 3, no. 2, 1966, pp. 101-136.

Sandhu, Kernial Singh., 'Tamil and other Indian Convicts in the Straits Settlements AD. 1790–1873', *Proceedings of the First International*

Conference of Tamil Studies, Kuala Lumpur, 1968, vol. 1, pp. 197–208.

__________, *Indians in Malaya, Immigration and Settlement (Some Aspects of their Migration and Settlement)* Cambridge, 1969.

Sastri, Nilakanta., *The Colas*, Madras, 1984.

Shamugam, P., 'Brahmadeyas in the Pallava Country', in S. Rajagopal, ed., *Kaveri: Studies in Epigraphy, Archaeology and History*, Chennai, 2001, pp. 331-342.

Singaravelou, *Les Indien de la Guadeloupe*, Thesis Bordeaux III, 1975.

Singaravelou, *Les Indiens de la Caraibe*, III vols., Paris, 1987.

Sivasubramanian, Aa., *Brahmahaththi: Varalaarum Vazhakkaarum*, Chennai, 2008.

__________, *Brahaamana Bhojanamum Satti Sorrum: Idaikaala Thamizhagathil Vaithigamum Saathi Uruvakkamum*, 2017.

Srinivas, M.D., T.G Paramasivam and T. Pushkal, *Thirupporur and Vadakupattu: Eighteenth Century Locality Accounts*, Chennai, 2001.

Stein, Burton., *Peasant State and Society in Medieval South India*, Delhi, 1980.

Stephen, S. Jeyaseela., *The Coromandel Coast and its Hinterland: Economy, Society and Political System, 1500-1600*, Delhi, 1997.

__________, *Portuguese in the Tamil Coast: Historical Explorations in Commerce and Culture, 1507-1749*, Pondicherry, 1998.

__________, *The Land, Peasantry and Peasant Life in India: New Direction and Renewed Debate*, Manak Publications, New Delhi, 2008.

__________, *Expanding Portuguese Empire and the Tamil Economy: Sixteenth-Eighteenth Centuries*, Delhi, 2009.

__________, *Oceanscapes: Tamil Textiles in the Early Modern World*, Delhi, Primus, 2014.

__________, *A Meeting of the Minds: European and Tamil Encounters in Modern Sciences, 1507-1857*, Delhi, Primus, 2016.

__________, ed., *The Hearbeat of a Missionary: Letters and Reports of Louis Savinien Dupuis in Pondicherry, 1839-74*, Pondicherry, 2017.

__________, *The First Catholic Bible in Tamil and Louis Savinien Dupuis at Pondicherry: A History of Translation and Printing, 1850-7*, Pondicherry, 2017.

__________, *Missioner Tamil: Written and Printed in Pondicherry: Literature and Louis Savinien Dupuis, 1841-73*, Pondicherry, 2017.

__________, *Thamizh Makkal Varalaaru: Kaalaniya Thodakkakaalam*, Chennai, 2018.

__________, *Pondicherry under the French: Illuminating the Urban Landscape*, Delhi, Primus, 2018.

Subramanian, T.N., 'Pallankoil Jaina Cooper-Plate Grant of Early Pallava Period', *Transactions of the Archaeological Society of South India*, 1958-59, vol. IV, pp. 41-83.

Teelock, Vijayalakshmi., *Mauritius Indentured Labour and Society, 1835-1935*, Moka, 2001.

__________, ed., *The Vagrant Depot of Grand River: Its Surroundings and Vagrancy in British Mauritius*: Port Louis, 2004.

Tinker Hugh., *A New System of Slavery: The Export of Indian Labour Overseas, 1830-1920*, London, 1974.

Tirumalai, R., 'The Brahmadyeas of Pudukottai District', in R. Tirumalai, *Collected Papers: Studies in South Indian Epigraphy and History (of land organization, development and accounts and select Chola and Pandyan townships)*, Madras, 1994, pp. 162-176.

Tomich, W. Dale., *Slavery in the Circuit of Sugar: Martinique and the World Economy, 1830-1848*, Johns Hopkins University Press, Baltimore, 1990.

Vedachalam, N., *Society and Culture of Pandya Nadu Gleaned from Literature and Inscriptions*, Ph.D. Dissertation, Tamil University, 1993.

Weber, Jacques., *Les Etablissements français en Inde au XIXe Siècle (1816-1914),* Paris, 5 vols, Paris, 1988.

__________, 'L'emigration indienne a` La Reunion: 'Contraire a` la morale' ou 'utile a` l'humanite'? (1829–1860)', in *Esclavage et abolitions dans l'ocean Indien, 1723–1860*, ed., Edmond Maestri, Paris, L'Harmattan, 2002, pp. 300–10.

Weerakoon, R., *The Evolution of Labour Law in Sri Lanka: Tea Plantation to Free Trade Zone*, Colombo, 1986.

Wenzlhuemer, Roland., 'Indian Labour Immigration and British Labour Policy in Nineteenth-Century Ceylon', *Modern Asian Studies*, vol. 41, no. 3, 2007, pp. 575–602.

Wickers, Lucien., *L'immigration reglementee a Ile de la Reunion*, Doctoral thesis, Paris, 1911.

Wurtzburg, C.E., *Raffles of the Eastern Isles*, Oxford University Press, Singapore, 1954.

Yang, Anand., 'Indian Convict Workers in Southeast Asia in the Late Eighteenth and Early Nineteenth Centuries', *Journal of World History*, vol. 14, no. 2, 2003, pp. 179-208.

Index

C

D

E

F

T